a look at the micro-nation
of home for new moms

Home Inspired

By

Naomi Bloom

Home Inspired

A look into the micro-nation of home for new moms

By Naomi Bloom

Edited by Hannah Roark, Danielle Anderson
Cover design by Mary Fournier

ISBN: 978-0-692-18866-8

This work is published by Home Inspired Publishing

P.O. Box 781401
Wichita, KS 67278
http://homeinspired.org

If you would like to contact the author or are interested in translating the material, please email naomi@homeinspired.org.

Foreword

I was born in 1950. During the late '60s and early '70s women's lib came into vogue. Along with many women of my generation, there was a lot of questioning about our role as women and an interest in expanding the boundaries and restrictions that society placed on women. I met my husband-to-be, Chris, in 1972. We married in 1976 and have been together ever since. I started working as a professional musician right out of college and was a member of the St. Louis Symphony violin section for 43 years. Chris was always clear that he wanted children, but I had many fears about becoming a mother. A lot of my fears revolved around handling pregnancy and motherhood while working in a demanding profession. I thought long and hard before becoming pregnant; I even joined a discussion group with other women contemplating the same choice.

I finally decided I wanted to have a baby. The pregnancy, birth, and the first year were all difficult for me. I felt exhausted and depleted but returned to work after my maternity leave was over and tried to manage everything. After getting through the first year, things got somewhat easier. After a while, Chris and I started thinking about having another baby, but I was still conflicted and fearful. After several miscarriages, I knew that I really wanted another baby, and six years after Naomi was born, Ariel came along. The whole experience of the pregnancy, birth, and first year were much easier for me the second time around. We were blessed to have two bright, beautiful, healthy, and talented girls. Chris and I cherished our daughters and tried our best to be good parents. Somehow, there was always healthy, good food on the table, and we encouraged our girls' interests and talents. Like many working mothers, I often felt stressed, tired, and pulled in too many directions. I also harbored resentment that running the household landed more heavily on my shoulders, even though Chris and I both had the same work schedule (he was also in the Symphony). As our girls grew up, what I wanted for them was to be happy, fulfilled, and to have a way to support themselves.

It has been a joy to see Naomi become a wonderful mother and for Chris and I to be blessed with two beautiful, bright grandchildren. I am glad that Naomi is able to be a full-time mom, and I can see how our grandchildren benefit from all the loving attention they receive from both their parents. I am grateful that Naomi was able to make this choice to stay at home with her children during their young years. I know it is not always easy to be with young children so many hours of the day, and I respect and honor the terrific job she is doing.

Deborah Bloom, Naomi's mom

Introduction

"If you miss the season, you miss the moment."
– Havillah Cunnington

"Your success as a family and our success as a society, depends not on what happens in the White House but on what happens inside your house."
– Barbara Bush

I've never gone through such an extreme season change as I did when I became a first-time mom. In the beginning of my motherhood journey, I was disoriented and felt like the landscape was rather bleak. What is a woman to do when she lands on "Mars" (my description of motherhood)? Many abandon ship or look to shape their new scenery into something that looks like their old familiar territories. We can try to cram motherhood into spaces that we understand, or we can settle down and settle in and begin to explore this new world.

As I began to look around, I realized that there were uncharted wonders to be discovered on Mars. There are unseen moments behind closed doors that are mundane and yet glorious.

As I began to settle into my new world, I realized that my heart was shifting and changing in beautiful ways that I never knew I needed.

This book comes from my initial exploration of Mars. I hope that it encourages and imparts grace to anyone who is shifting seasons and launching into motherhood. I hope that it adds a sense of wonder and awe at God's intent for home. And I hope it brings you, mom, wherever you are, into the moment so you don't miss it! There you will flourish. There you will find sustenance and glory. There you will be transformed to love and be loved more and more.

Love,

Naomi

Table of Contents

Chapter 1

Foundations

These first two essays are foundational for the rest of this book. They lay the groundwork ideas for everything else. They were written during the first few months of my motherhood journey.

1.0

Love looks like something and often that something is small. *

In the movie, *Men in Black*, the whole tension of the plot is about who will find the "universe." There are aliens desperately leaving planet Earth because they think the universe is going to be turned over to the hands of evil rulers. On his deathbed in the morgue, the steward of the universe said, gasping for air, "The universe is in Orion's belt." Turns out, he was talking about a cat named Orion who had a charm on his collar which held the universe. But Will Smith, the main hero, didn't understand what his final words meant. He was looking for something big, something expansive, something vast and comprehensive. He was rebuked by another alien, "Why do you humans always think that important things have to be big?"

Sometimes, we can't see what we are looking for because our expectation is wrong.

I can so relate to Will Smith's mistake. When I became a follower of Jesus, I was told that I was a world-changer. I believed it and realized that my purpose and destiny mattered for the sake of history and the planet. I imagined doing something BIG, something that would make a huge splash in the world for Christ, something that would get recognition for how much good it added to the world. I was willing to do whatever it took: preach open air on campus, be radical, travel to different nations... big stuff.

But then I found myself on "Mars." Motherhood threw me for a total loop. On Mars, everything is tiny. Tiny shoes. Tiny hands. Tiny hats. Tiny words like "goo."

Some people find this small world delightful. But the tiny world of Mars really frustrated me most of the time. It seemed that my life was reduced to tiny actions: a smile when our son looked my way, a word like "no" when he was about to go to a dangerous place, a diaper here, a bottle there. Tiny actions filled up my days and my nights, and quite honestly, I found it disheartening and disillusioning. It felt oh-so-small and insignificant compared to the big, vast impact I thought I was called to make.

Consequently, I had a crisis of significance.

See, no one had ever explained to me the value system of Mars. The value system of Mars differs from the way of Earth. The way of Earth says that one has to accomplish something big, have a huge title, gain lots of power, and make lots of money to have an impact. The way of Mars is in the details. On Mars, one impacts the world through thousands of tiny, seemingly insignificant details done in love. It's by choosing to lay down one's life that one has an impact on the world of Mars.

Hmm. Mars sounds a lot like the way of the Kingdom. *Wink wink, nudge nudge.*

So, if I was slowly learning the way of the Kingdom on my new planet, then why was my mind insisting that what I was doing was so insignificant? **I'd been looking for significance outside these small actions.**

I'd been had!! Whoever said those little acts of love were insignificant? In fact, the most beautiful works of art are a compilation of small brush strokes or stitches. There is beauty in the compilation of many, small, intentional contributions to a project. Often, the glory of something is in the details. Whoever said that there was no glory in the tiny things?

I'd been duped. I was looking for significance outside these small actions. Meanwhile it was through the tiny actions, the tiny exchanges, the tiny moments of communicating love in a thousand ways that I had the opportunity to create my magnum opus.

And I almost missed it entirely. I almost missed a huge chunk of my calling. I'd almost found a flight off Mars and gone on to do the "BIG" things. For the first part of my son Judah's life, I fought for position and title in the "important" meetings, missing the value of the simple exchanges with him, wanting to hire them out. Then I realized that God many times shows up in a manger. I almost forsook this great opportunity to weave a breathtaking tapestry because I couldn't see the glory in the small, simple things.

I resolved to stick it out, at least another day, at least another week, maybe another month. Stick it out and let the wisdom of Mars dawn on me gradually as I slowed down enough to see the value of the tiny.

And here I am: still on Mars, still putting my hand to the simple and the mundane, still at times trying to find significance, still reminding myself daily that the small things matter, still dying to myself daily, still endeavoring to love well. And meanwhile, I'm finding the treasures of God's Kingdom in the tiny ways of Mars.

Ask the Holy Spirit to reveal the small ways He demonstrates His love to you each day.

*The title partially came from a quote from missionary Heidi Baker who says, "Love looks like something."

1.1

The home is a micro-nation with incredible world-changing potential.

I flopped down on our bed after being awake for what seemed like two continual months. My husband and I were in the throes of adjusting to our first kid, Judah. I peered through sleepy eyes out of the bedroom door and looked at our banister. It was draped with blankets and garments. We kept the clean ones there as a holding place before they went into our son's room. The pattern was, wait until he's asleep and then frantically get as much as possible done before he wakes. So, anything that had to go into his room had a holding place on the bannister. I thought, "Those blankets need to be pushed through the system and land in Judah's closet."

And then it dawned on me: a house, just like a society, has systems!

Here's the background on that...

I became a Christian in 2000 during my senior year of college. At that time, God made His love and His Lordship very real to me. I was integrated into current Christian culture which was, by and large, very church centered. What I mean is that the whole emphasis of most churches was to get people into relationship with God and then have those people turn around and help others get into relationship with God. Not bad, but not the full picture.

In 2009, my tight group of friends and I started to realize that the Gospel has much more pervasive implications than just growing big, thriving churches. The Gospel is, by its very nature, a culture changer. The Gospel of the Kingdom is the good news of God's redemptive, merciful, and just reign coming into every area of life: economics, arts, business, medicine, development, education, etc. We began to see that God wants to impact all areas of life and that all of life is sacred. Our eyes were opened to the world-changing nature of the Gospel.

This was all fun and games until I landed myself at home in this mommy gig. It felt small and mundane. It felt arduous and honestly quite boring at times: the endless diapers, dishes, laundry, dirt, the poop, the pee, the messy eating times, the messy beds. I could hardly keep up and honestly had very little vision for what I was doing in life other than just trying to survive. I felt that I had been removed from the real world-changing efforts me and my colleagues were conceiving and I was now relegated to the place of a maid. It was a pretty depressed time for me.

Back to the bed...

In that moment, in my dazed state, I realized the connection between home and society, society and home. The home is the miniature version of the larger society. Every home contributes in one way or another to the larger civilization just as building blocks do to a building. As the strength of collective homes in a society go, so goes the strength of the society. I suddenly had a glimpse of a wondrous miniature nation, and the great thing was, I had creative rights with my husband to form this nation's culture.

A home has systems just as society has systems. Ideas drive the systems in a home just as ideas drive the systems in a society. The home has an economy, a government, a culture, food supply, imports, exports, a health care system, a waste management system, etc. These systems all work together to create some kind of functioning home, just as they all work together to create some kind of functioning nation or state or city.

Some homes echo the culture of the world. For example, for many homes in America, their economy is based on debt. Want a new toy? Just pay for it with credit. Well, debt is the basis for our nation's economy and many homes contribute heartily to this culture.

But we have, if we see it and choose to embrace it, this grand opportunity to intentionally build an alternative, kingdom culture in our home for the glory of our God and Christ. We have the opportunity to build a culture of love, of beauty, of justice, of righteousness, of service, of honor, of sacrifice, of generational transfer... a God kind of culture in and through the systems of our home. I started to perk up as I realized that I had complete freedom to run this domain in a way that honors my God. A sense of significance and creativity started to percolate in my heart as I caught a vision for designing and cultivating my very own "garden" at home.

I have very little power over the presidential election results, the systemic lust pervasive in our nation, the greed and hate that drive many of the world's biggest superpowers. But here in my own home, within the boundaries of these four walls, I have authority (along with my husband) to make something beautiful and to train up little disciples to perpetuate that same beauty. What an incredible opportunity and what a need in this world to have Kingdom oases: real, honest places where people are endeavoring in their imperfect yet sincere quest to bring Heaven to Earth right in the context of their very homes.

Could I make a sanctuary where the orphan, the widow, and the stranger could come and find comfort and warmth? Could I make the living Word, the law of the land in my home? Could I make a place where people might find restoration? Could I make a place where my family would have peace and joy and transparency? Suddenly, there was a synthesis of my big, grand Kingdom revelation and the small tasks I found myself doing day and in and out. I had the opportunity to prayerfully and artfully weave heaven into my home in increasing intensity day after day. In that moment, I took ownership of something that seemed hard and yet doable, not just an ideal anymore. And my hope was that maybe as others entered into my created Kingdom space, they would taste and see a good God there.

Just as the queen of Sheba came to King Solomon's house and marveled at the systems and ways of his house, so too I wondered if I could make a place where people knew that a God of all wisdom and goodness informed its inception, development, and ongoing sustainment. The creation of a space and a place like this felt like maybe one of the most important tasks I might ever do in my lifetime.

I hadn't seen it before. In the throes of trying to change the world "out there," I had neglected the possibility of home. And in that moment, lying on the bed, I had a glimpse of the potential greatness in home. I caught a genesis of revelation about home that could and would rock my understanding and my perspective about building a "home inspired": a home that lives and breathes by the wisdom of God… Maybe I should be sleep deprived more often.

Ask the Holy Spirit for creative insight into how He wants to form and fashion your home inspired.

Chapter 2

Mom's heart: the life blood of home inspired

I can look only as far as myself for much of what is required to make my home inspired. It's so easy to look "out there." I can think, "My home would really be inspired if only that couch fit in that awkward space or that kid had a better attitude." But if we are honest, as our heart goes, so goes the tone and atmosphere of home. So, I can't start this book any other way than with honest confessions and stories from my own broken journey toward having a heart that continually flows with Kingdom reality. As Stephen Mansfield says, "Culture is what is allowed to grow." How do I guard and cultivate my heart so that I grow Kingdom culture within and without? These essays draw from that journey in my life.

2.0

Significance does not come from what we do, it comes from whose we are.

There was one,
When I was young,
Who knew my heart,
He knew my sorrow.
He held my hand.
And he led me to trust Him.
– United Pursuit "Hidden"

In college at The University of Kansas, I sought God. I wanted to know Him for who He really is and when I found the man Christ Jesus, my life was forever changed. I made it my aim to live a life worthy of His sacrifice.

And I pursued that end with all my heart, but I found myself regularly stumbling over the same stone. I was a woman in a church culture where women often found their world-changing significance from things like marriage, children, and homeschooling. No one outright said any of that. But looking around as a young Christian, the undercurrents were forceful and clear: I needed these titles to truly fulfill my God-designed purpose.

So, I tried to fill that post. I sought for years to find the right guy, settle down, and have a family. But *that* story, *my* story for *my* life, didn't seem to materialize. And so, my matter meter started to tremble near low. What happens if I never marry? Do I still matter? Does God have something for me despite my single status?

My matter meter drove me into God and into personal crisis simultaneously. I fought and wrangled for a "place at that table" that seemed to matter. I wasn't going to be left out because I was a woman! I scrapped and scraped for validation in the church culture. And some of that was good. I felt at times that I was fighting for all women and in some ways, I was. It was true that many women had been sidelined from leadership into boxy, religious, man-made designs. I made it my personal mission to fight for women to be able to contribute to our church culture in a wider, deeper way.

But for me, the fight was laced with insecurity, fear, and anxiety. I felt many times like I was begging someone to give me a mark of approval. Quite often, I felt that I was begging God for that same mark. It was a difficult time.

Then, my title changed from campus minister and minister of women to wife and mom. And in a moment, or over the course of a few years, I was positioned very differently amongst my friends. I had the titles that supposedly brought fulfillment and significance and yet I still felt the same anxiety about insignificance and the need for title and approval. My situation had changed but my heart had not.

He met me in that dark, desperate place over and over again. He met me in my sorrow and insecurity. And He slowly led me step by step down the road. I had no idea how blind I was. I had no idea how small my estimation of His love really was. He taught me little by little, with patience and gentility, that my value never comes from what I do or what title I hold: minister, world-traveler, single, married, mom, etc. Like a lover sitting beside their beloved as they recover from sickness, God sat beside me and held water up to my mouth so I could drink. I was sick with performance, with religion, and with man-pleasing. And through it all, He drew me into His love.

He was the constant in all the various life phases and situations. He was constantly working on something of which I was fairly oblivious.

He was leading me to conclude that my value comes from being made in His image and is revealed only as I worship the One who is worthy in every season and every phase of life. He met me in the darkness, never shaming me for my blindness, only dropping light in bits and pieces before me so that I could handle it.

The whole time that I wrestled with God's intention for women in the church and God's heart for me as a woman, He was doing something else. The entire time I felt the sting of loneliness in my singlehood and isolation after I'd had our first child, He was doing something else. He was drawing me into His tenderness. I was looking for definition, answers, scriptural principles, recognition, significance. But He was leading me to lean on His chest, trust His love, trust His heart. In all the fight and in all the struggle, he had one thing in mind: "Naomi, I want you to know Me. I want you to know my heart for you. I want you to be so secure in this that you can have a place at the most illustrious table one day and then be home folding clothes for the next year and be okay with both of those assignments."

I can never say that I've arrived. But He's led me to trust Him more. And as I trust, I see His blessings unfold layer by layer.

Do you struggle to find your significance from what you do? Ask the Holy Spirit for insight about where your significance truly comes from.

2.1

We have to experience grace in order to give it away.

Coffee shop. Coffee, small treat. Laptop opened. Instrumentals in my ears. Reset time.

I first type in my journal, "God I really need Your help right now."

How do I reset after a day where I've lost my cool more than once with my precious child who happens to be sick? After a day where I've gotten that strained tone of voice, the one that wants a piece of control or, if I'm honest, all control over what is happening? After I've put my little, dumb, insignificant project in front of my main prizes in life?

How do I reset?

I'm stalling. I'm de-frazzling as I write the words on this page.

I just need a little time to feel the sadness of the misses. I just need a little moment to come to my Father and talk to him about my disappointments. I just need a little moment to get some comfort that I haven't thoroughly messed it all up with the mess-ups of today.

Bite one of the almond butter cup. I allow it to melt between my tongue and roof of my mouth. It's comforting. A treat defining this reset space.

"I will sing of lovingkindness and justice, to You, O Lord, I will sing praises. I will give heed to the blameless way. When will You come to me? I will walk within my house in the integrity of my heart." Psalm 101:1-2 NASB

I remind myself that I am a woman of integrity; one who is the righteousness of God in Christ. One who wants to do the right thing. Sensitive enough to know I've missed it. *Thank You, Lord.*

Bite two. I try to savor it, knowing that I don't have unlimited supply or unlimited time.

"I will set no worthless thing before my eyes; I hate the work of those who fall away; It shall not fasten its grip on me. A perverse heart shall depart from me; I will know no evil..." Psalm 101:3-4 NASB

I choose to lay my outbursts, my messes at the cross. I will not pick up the whip and beat myself for my mistakes. These are worthless things. His new mercy always triumphs my petty judgements.

Now the radio is talking straight to me: "What if you could go back to one day, redo your mistakes? ... Love's never been a lost cause." I am not a lost cause. Our family is not a lost cause.

One almond cup down. One to go. The momentum of hope has increased. My focus intensifies. I know where I'm headed now.

"He who practices deceit shall not dwell within my house; He who speaks falsehood shall not maintain his position before me. Every morning I will destroy all the wicked of the land, so as to cut off from the city of the Lord all those who do iniquity." Psalm 101:7-8 NASB

I laugh uproariously (and a little forcedly) at the lie of the accuser saying that my relationship with God is based on my performance and that my failures disqualify me. HAHAHA!!! Fake laughter, but true that those lies are worthy of a chuckle. The laughter disarms the lies that mock me. It mocks them and releases their threat from me. I'm working to be on truth's side, working to abide, and boldness is rising. I am a much-loved child at my worst. On my absolute worst day, I am a much-loved child.

Any apps of condemnation running in the background, I cancel! Clear the mechanism, reset. I walk by grace through faith. His Spirit empowers me.

And then I hear not just the scriptures I know, but I hear Him.

"Naomi, you are covered by love. I love you. Love covers a multitude of sin."

"Lord I re-consecrate my mind, my heart, my hands, my body, my will to You."

"Thank you, Naomi, thank you really. But even if you never did that, I could never stop my feelings for you."

"Lord, what are your feelings for me?"

"You are my bride, stunning and righteous, beautiful and limping still in places. You are becoming everything I always imagined through my love. My hope over you is unwavering. You are not there yet and that is OKAY. Don't you think I knew that going into this marriage?"

Tears well. Last bite. Definitive. Satisfying and yet good to be done.

"Let me flood your thinking when it comes to motherhood decisions. Every step toward me, I'm thrilled. Every step toward trusting in my voice, I'm thrilled. You are beautiful right now, and you are even more beautiful as we go down the road. I'm going with you. I'm helping you to get up again."

Reset now. Reset with His acceptance, knowing I'm loved so I can give love away. Reset with mercy experienced. Reset knowing I'm not alone.

How can I help but run home and scoop up my little one in my arms? How can I help but kiss him all over and tell him how much I love him, how proud I am of him? How can I help but be patient with him as he learns to obey? How can I help but celebrate even the littlest bit of improvement and growth? How can I help but just enjoy him right where he is and encourage him on in this journey toward his brilliant future? How can I help but give away this gorgeous grace I've been given?

Ask the Holy Spirit to give you an encounter with His grace right now.

2.2

Radical life as a disciple demands unconditional love and sacrifice.

When I first became a Christian, I prided myself on being radically all in. I looked around and it looked like those that were radical were brazenly outward about their faith; bold like lions in their witness.

So, I chose to emulate those qualities. I walked up to strangers to share Jesus. I preached "open air" out on campus. I gave my testimony anywhere and everywhere I had the opportunity. I boldly proclaimed Jesus! And I was applauded by Christians for my boldness.

Then, when I became a mom, a lot of that type of activity stopped or significantly slowed. And although I felt I was learning nothing at times, and not growing at all, I was actually growing exponentially in things like sacrificial love and servanthood (not two of my strengths going into the game).

The thing is, those two qualities aren't so applauded in Christian circles because, for the most part, they aren't publicly seen. And honestly, my value for these characteristics was pretty low. So, while I continued to grow, I felt my "radical" title fade as I retreated into a secret place serving one little person most of the time.

But recently, while waiting in line to pick up Chick-fil-A, I had this thought: "The meaning of 'radical' actually comes from the idea of root." The first definition for radical on Dictionary.com is "of or going to the root of origin: fundamental."

If I'm a real radical Christian, and not just living for the praises of man, I will go back to the fundamental roots of my belief system: and that would be, um... Jesus. And let me tell you, Jesus was bold like a lion but also gentle like a lamb. Jesus majored in servanthood and takes the cake for sacrificial love!

The radical root of my faith is love in all of its boldness and gentility because God is love. And while I was doing my best to zealously express my love for God, I had a lot of growing to do in the areas of love that are more thankless.

As I delved even deeper into my understanding of this, I started to realize that in the pre-mom radical years, my radical love for God was shown in "doing" lots of things for Him. But as I graduated into momhood, it became much more about being. It became about being a manifestation of love to the little ones. Of course, there was a lot of doing, but the real love came in being present with them as God is continually present with us.

So, although I am not seen so much by people nor applauded so much by the crowds for my "radical" commitment to Christ, my roots are actually going deeper into the character of Christ. And as I sit with Him and take my cues from being with Him, I'm able to translate his way of love to those around me. My root system is forming itself to look a little more like His!

I guess I'm more radical these days than I was before, even if no one sees but Him.

Ask the Holy Spirit to reveal how your roots are going down deeper into the character of Christ these days.

2.3

Self-pity separates us from God and all the resources of heaven.

Over the summer, my small family of 3.5 (three people plus one on the way) took what I would call a monumental road trip to the East Coast. At the onset, I was very excited to see old friends and encounter new cities with my husband and our almost three-year-old. I looked forward to archiving a whole new set of experiences together. But as the trip rolled on and the moving from house to house, from environment to environment, from crappy fast food to crappy fast food, also marched on, let me tell you, it got a little more real for me.

I started to get really tired of the road. And I began to agree with some really nasty lies.

These lies were particularly rooted in victimhood. I felt victimized by our plans. I felt victimized by other people's schedules. I felt victimized by my son. I felt victimized by my husband.

And I began to complain, at first a little and then a lot. The thing was, I felt completely justified in complaining because many of my most basic needs were not being met very well.

My sweet husband was doing everything he knew to help me and support me acknowledging that I was pregnant and that this wasn't easy.

But by the time we were at the end of trip, it was never enough for me, and he was tired too. So, he said, "Okay, enough! I'll do anything to get you to stop complaining."

This was a complete wake-up call because my husband hardly ever says things like this. He is great at taking responsibility for his attitudes and actions most of the time, regardless of other people's choices. But in this moment, the truth of the effects of my ugliness came out and he was honest.

It was a sobering moment for me. I began to wake up from what felt like such a justifiably long pity party. I began to wake up from my victimized mindset and I began to apologize. I also began to thank my husband and thank God for all the ways He had extended grace to me on the trip, extensions of grace that I could not see until rightfully being humbled. And I began to feel contentedness return to my being.

Meanwhile, God was showing me that these victim mindsets had infected my attitude pretty consistently even before the trip. I could usually lift myself out of it, but that's different from building an immunity to it. I never had so clearly identified it until this trip.

So, I went home and began to intentionally work on mind renewal. I saw with such clarity that this attitude and these thought patterns were my enemies, not my husband, not my son, not my life's circumstances. I started to really be aware that I could choose to thrive in any given circumstance. When I would start to feel sorry for myself, neglected or whatever, I realized it really wasn't an accusation against my husband so much as an accusation against God. It's the accusation that God hasn't given me what I need, that I don't have a good provider and that I'm all alone. It's the accusation that would cause me to create some kind of consensus with myself or with others that my situation sucked and that God wasn't truly taking care of me. And I could find people who would agree with me about that. I started to see that my issue wasn't my circumstances or relationships. My issue was blindness, lack of faith, to see what God had already provided for me.

It's really the same lie that came to Eve in the garden. "Does God really care? Has He really provided everything you need? Can you really trust Him? Does He really love you and have your best in mind? I mean, look at the circumstances, the obvious answer is no. He is withholding the best from you."

Meanwhile, I got a new revelation about the curse that came upon Eve after her fall: Her desire would be for her husband and he would rule over her. I started to realize that I was looking with sad, pathetic eyes toward my husband to fill these needs I felt were unfulfilled. I was desiring him to fix my sad state, but, truth be told, he could never give enough to fill the void in me. It would never be enough from him because what I really needed only God could provide.

The sad part was that God had already provided it; I'd just fallen into a web of lies about my circumstances and situations. I agreed with the accuser about God and Him withholding from me, and therefore I cut myself off from all the great benefits of the cross and the incredibly expensive work of redemption. My faith eyes were blind. And all I could see was lack all around me.

I realized that self-pity totally robs me of problem solving, creativity, joy, and peace. It robs the moment of potential and possibility. It is like

Round-Up applied to the life-giving tree that is my faith in God. It's the quickest way for the enemy to separate my mind from God and all that he has made available to me in Christ.

I began to attack this infectious disease with truth. And let me tell you, what a makeover I've had!! The complaining stopped. If it starts to pop up, I now see it as the first fruits of my agreement with a lie. The gratitude grew. I can now see that if I am tempted to complain, I can will myself to switch into grateful mode. Out loud I speak the praises and great gifts of God. It's hard to accuse God when you see all that He's given you. The strain on my marriage ceased almost immediately. I no longer desired for him to fix my sad state. I know now that my world is full of great possibility and there is always a solution—even when I'm exhausted. And I started to really enjoy motherhood in a whole new way. No longer was I a victim to the highs and lows of my son's day. I was guarding my joy, peace, and gratitude and literally creating a beautiful garden with God in my heart. It is out of this garden that God began to grow fruit like never before, fruit that now my son and daughter get to enjoy.

Self-pity isn't something that everyone struggles with, but when faced with our most basic needs being denied, the enemy appeals to us with this lie. That's when we get to believe! We get to choose to thrive! We get to dig deep into our reservoirs of mental grit and hold to the truth. If we resist the enemy, he will flee. And as a result, our faithfulness to God and our ability to see Him in every circumstance will only grow.

Ask the Holy Spirit if you need to deal with any self-pity. Ask Him to show you how to thrive in this season.

2.4

God is committed to beautifying us from the inside out.

Imagine a seed floating low to the ground on a gentle, damp breeze until it lands on the fertile floor of a rainforest. This seed nestles its way into the loose earth and there finds all it needs to sprout and grow a green, healthy stalk. Over time it unfurls and buds and blooms. Its blossoms are a gorgeous pattern of purples and shimmery golds. This flower is stunning. Stretching out toward the few rays of sun that peek through the canopy in the day, this flower thrives and then, after some time, this flower, as all things on Earth do, withers and eventually goes back to the Earth from which it came.

This flower lived its entire life hidden from any acknowledgement of its beauty by the outside world. And this kind of thing happens all over God's creation: wildflowers on the Midwestern plains with their delicate diversity, birds in the Amazon rainforest with patchworks of brilliance in their feathers, mountain ranges tinseled with snow and ice installations. They all are spectacularly beautiful and yet are hidden from publicity and exist in seclusion.

For some time, I've been asking this question: "Lord, if no one sees these things, then **why** do you make them?"

My background is in the arts. My whole family has some kind of serious art commitment. My sister was a theater major, my parents were/are professional musicians, and as for me, I was a dance major. In the world of art, much of the purpose, "the why" for creating something, is for it to eventually be seen and enjoyed by others. One goes through cycle after cycle of ideating, formulating, and then producing only to culminate with a performance or show of some sort with lots of flowers and recognition, compliments, etc.

And isn't that how we often work as humans? We live for the show. We put all this effort into the moments of the day or week when we will be seen the most. We do this because we long for the approval and at least the recognition of our audience, whoever they are.

But God, in hiding these brilliant works, shows us something about Himself. His "why" must be different from most human artists because many times He will create incredibly beautiful things knowing, in His sovereignty, that they will never been seen by a human eye. So again, "Why, Lord, do you make them?"

I keep coming back to this answer: **it's because He cannot help it**. Those beautiful wonders come from Him: a beautiful God. They are created out of His integrous, unified self. His creation comes out of who He is, and He is beautiful, therefore His creations are beautiful, even if no one ever recognizes them as such. God isn't defined by what someone sees of Him. He just is, and it is up to us to investigate and discover this beautiful artist of old.

It is a human tendency and trap in our fallen state to live for the recognition and acknowledgement of others. We try to make our houses look perfect, we get plastic surgery, we act one way around our families in public and another at home, we smile and shake hands at church and then crumble at home. And we do all of these things because we know that there is "ugly" in our lives that we do not want others to see. It's driven by thick and thin layers of shame about who we really are.

For me, I was all about recognition in ministry. I wanted people to know how much I was doing to advance the Kingdom and I wanted them to recognize that it was important. Two years ago, we had a son and I was forced into a place of obscurity. In those places, one discovers the factions and fault lines in one's character. I was, unknowingly, an approval/affirmation addict. But being at home, very few recognized the virtues of the work I was doing as a mom and as a homemaker. Most people saw only about one percent of what I did in a day. At first, I went through approval withdrawals—I was detoxing. Then my heart started to see the beauty of this obscurity. It was forcing me to live for God alone. I was starting to live a life of integrity. My secret life was growing. And I was starting to enjoy the process.

God cares about our integrity and so do other people. They want to know that as they get closer to us and as they are some of the closest to us, it only gets better and better, that we, in essence, get more and more beautiful. This is only a work of the Holy Spirit in our lives. Apart from Him, we can try to cover the ugly for a while, but it will eventually be revealed. We can look neatly packaged on the outside but can be full of rottenness on the inside, and honestly, that's how we tend to want to stay.

But not God. He is more beautiful the more you explore, the more you pull back the layers. He is more beautiful because He is beauty and He can be nothing else! And He draws us into this way of life as well. He is wanting to beautify the humble with wholeness, strength, zeal, and layers of wisdom and love. And He will draw us away into the wilderness to speak tenderly to us about these things. The wilderness, somewhere deep in the rainforest, is where we meet a beautiful God making beautiful things and beautifying us in secret.

Ask the Holy Spirit to show you how He is beautifying you these days.

2.5

Love goes to the lowest and often most obscure places.

Recently my son Judah was sick. As most moms know, when a child gets sick at home, everything stops, the schedule grinds to a halt, and it's all about caring for that child who is crabby and not their usual. Meanwhile, there is little sleep, many demands, and less breaks than on a typical day. The isolation increases and the creative possibilities for the day decrease.

Kind of a dismal description, I know. But listen, it's real.

It's hard. And to make matters worse, I have this idea rattling around in my head that this is somehow slave labor in the name of motherhood having little or nothing to do with changing the world. Many of us want to change the world, but what does that really mean? It's a hard pill to swallow, but in God's kingdom, it often means slowing down for the lowest and the least.

Jesus said, "That which you do to the least of these, you do to Me."

I delude myself when I think that serving a sick Judah is slave labor because it's completely counter to this incredible King Jesus and His beautiful revolution. In my version of world-changing, I want to be in the important conversations, not wiping green snot from Judah's red nose. But where are the real frontlines of the battlefield? Are they not on the frontier of love? And does not love go to the least of these? Does not love go into the lowest places? Like a refreshing stream in a desert, love runs down. Love goes low.

In all of my pride and sense of self-importance, have I forgotten the way of love? Or am I simply being trained to have a greater capacity to change the world by expanding my love-bearing load?

Am I being trained to hang in there when love is not self-gratifying? To hang in there when love doesn't feel important? To hang in there when love feels lonely? To hang in there when love feels boring?

These are the intensive trainings for the elite Kingdom force that goes lower still. This is truly not for the faint of heart. It requires being present. It requires denying self. It requires dedication.

The King wants me.

The King wants YOU. But are you ready for the training that will make you ready to love extravagantly without asking anything in return? It's world-changing and yet mostly us-changing.

Ask the Holy Spirit to show you how He is training you to love more.

2.6

Maturity is required to handle the harvest of good seeds we sow.

When I prayed that prayer to get married, when I told God that I wanted a child, when I took actions that would make that a reality, I made choices, I sowed seeds that would eventually change my life forever. At first it didn't seem like anything was changing. At first it didn't seem like my hope for change was even heard by the only One who could make that happen. But as time went on, it happened. We conceived.

For many, the point of conception marks a huge shift in thinking: planning, preparation, imagining the future. Not so much for me. I really didn't know what that seed living within me meant.

I really had no idea how much my choice to sow a seed and to conceive would change my life until Judah came. And when he came, it all changed. It all changed because that seed needed me to constantly tend to him. That seed needed me to reorient my life around him. That seed wasn't just a nice idea. That seed changed everything.

And I cannot say that I was always grateful for that seed. I cannot say that I constantly remembered that I chose to conceive that seed way back when I prayed and released. I can honestly say that at times, I resented that seed and I resented the new life that seed had carried me into. I can honestly say that at times, being a garden tender for this one seed was boring, and at times, I felt like a prisoner to that seed and his wants and needs.

But... over time, I've started to see that that seed has taught me more about love than I ever thought I needed to know. That seed has brought more joy to more people, including me, than I ever thought imaginable. That seed has taught me more about what it means to really live and to really be fruitful and cultivate the Earth than any other person in my life. That seed has begun to confront my idols of control, self-preservation, and performance. That seed has begun to teach me that the greatest honor of my life is to leave a legacy beyond my time on Earth.

Unless a seed falls to the ground and dies, it cannot bear fruit. What if in the process of bearing fruit, the parts of me that needed to fall to the ground and die actually did (or are at least breathing their last breaths)?

So, now I'm working to own the choices that got me here. Often I think to myself, "How did I get here? This is so disorienting. What am I doing with my life? What did I do today? What did I do yesterday or the day before?"

When I made those powerful choices to pray and to sow seed so many years back, I made choices to reap in the way I'm currently reaping. And while the reaping is challenging and frustrating at times, I have to believe that right now I'm currently sowing other kinds of seed: words, prayers, actions, quiet service that I will reap in the next five, ten, twenty years of my life, and hopefully, even in eternity.

Ask the Holy Spirit to show you moments in your life when you had to mature because of good seeds you'd sown.

* * *

So, mom, or mother-to-be, you are reaping what you've sown. Now what? How do you want to live out your days as a mom? How now do you want to sow? Do you want your home to be saturated with Kingdom reality? How are you caring for the garden of your heart? Are you willing to allow the King to saturate your inner world and raise up His kind of fruit in and through you and your family? Are you willing to let Him orient you so that you see things through His eyes? The truth is, even your feeble "yes" is enough for Him to take you on this journey because He wants you to see this assignment through His eyes much more than you do. Say "yes" and enter beyond the wardrobe with me into a wonder-filled world where dynasties are created and magical moments are found in the mundane. Enter with me into the wonderful world of home.

Chapter 3

Home-Inspired Culture

Culture is what we allow to grow. We get to choose. We get to be intentional about how we build. I hope this chapter gets your wheels turning and conversations started with your spouse and friends regarding how you will steward this incredible opportunity to build Kingdom culture at home.

3.0

Home-Inspired culture is gloriously mundane.

Yesterday my son and I attended our first ever class at the zoo. Funny enough, it was me, my two-year-old son, and two teachers! I'm sure he felt a little triple-teamed. But everyone else was missing out because we were the only ones who got to learn about the wondrous life of bees. You might already know all this, but it was news to me. The bee digs into the flower to get pollen, and as he does, he gets pollen all over his hairy body. It's like pixy dust. The pollen is disseminated to the different flowers by the bees, thus pollinating the plants and trees and giving us fruit. The bees communicate with wagging and dancing. The bees create honey in their mouths and store it in the hive.

As we listened, I was launched into a state of worship. God's systems and designs are simple and brilliant works of art. There is order, productivity, communication, and economy. There is a relationship with the outside world. It's fascinating and amazing! It's one little part of a brilliantly designed and sustained ecosystem, and it happens every day, all day long, right before our eyes. Brilliance shrouded in the mundane.

Every day we wake up and go about our days, and every day bees have this wondrous little world that I would never know about had I not enrolled to take a dinky little class at the zoo.

I started thinking about "home" in light of our recent bee education. Within healthy homes, as within the life of bees, are these exquisite systems, delicately balanced, and beautifully designed. These systems bring life and fruit wherever they go. They perpetuate strength, honor, joy, and righteousness for generations.

It's gloriously mundane every time my son masters a new skill or memorizes a verse or learns to be kind and gentle with his hands. It's gloriously mundane when I don't lose my temper after one of his full-on meltdowns. It's gloriously mundane when I humble myself and apologize after I do lose my temper. It's gloriously mundane when my husband and I hug and show that we care about one another in front of our son. It's gloriously mundane when our home runs with order and joy and peace for most of the day. Haha! It's the glorious in the mundane.

The glorious in the mundane does not stop with being a mom. It's the dad who makes those little financial decisions putting his kids and family first each time. It's the building of a home, creative layer upon layer adding beauty, order, functionality, and design. It's caring for the neighbor who is new to the neighborhood. It's saving throughout the year for a getaway with the family. It's the grandmother who comes and gives freely of her time. It's the grandfather who honors and encourages and gives perspective to a discouraged dad.

These often aren't regarded as spectacular because they are everywhere and happen behind closed doors. But God's glory rests in the ecosystem where honor is air and in the habitat where love and humility reign. This is a pretty awe-inspiring thing that happens in little pockets all over the world in stories, mostly untold.

Ask the Holy Spirit to show you how he weaves the glorious into the mundane in your life.

3.1

Home-inspired culture is built on covenant as a vessel for intimacy and blessing.

Covenant, noun: to come; a coming together; a meeting or agreement of minds.

My husband and I have a unique story. He was married to my best friend and then she passed away. Fast forward one year, and in the very abridged version, after grieving for a season, we fell for one another and got married. We had been married for about a year and a half, trying to get pregnant the entire time, and living in Kansas City, pioneering a campus ministry when an interesting question came to a head. The question, for me, was about the nature of our relationship with his first wife's family as a married couple. Throughout our dating season and first year of marriage, I had a very ambivalent attitude about it all. To me it felt like a lot of work to include them in our lives in a familial way. In my head, I thought it involved lots of obligation without much benefit. I had no idea how much their lives would bless ours to this day.

One weekend, Austin (my husband) and I were visiting her father and step-mom. This weekend, my ambivalence was particularly acute. In between tears, I told Austin about it and he asked me to make the call, he would follow whatever I wanted. Great. Now if I chose to grow apart, I was the bad guy.

So, the next morning I got raw and real with God. I started to ask Him for clarity about the issue. He said it was a choice about whether we were going to grow apart over time or grow together over time. I saw, in one mental picture, two lines that started moving away from each other as they progressed across the page. In the other picture, I saw two lines that moved toward one another. I knew I needed to make a choice.

See, there is no middle ground. Relationships either grow apart or grow together. My inner turmoil came as a result of my lack of decision. I had not yet decided if we would walk in covenant or not. Isn't that the case with couples who live together for years, sleep together, even have kids together but never make the choice to marry? They are living in a perpetual state of ambivalence.

Recently, covenant has been on my mind. Covenant is so central to the social health of a nation. And really, covenant comes down to the simple illustration above. It is a choice to always grow together. This sounds simple, but obviously, given the divorce rate, is not as simple as one might initially think. Covenant requires humility, self-control, honesty, vulnerability, patience, kindness, forgiveness... in other words, covenant requires a love choice that is made once and is enforced each day after that.

Why don't we choose covenant? We worry that there is something better out there, that we'll get sick of the people we chose. We worry that we will have to give up some of our ways or that we will be hurt really badly. We worry that we aren't able to do it. But really, all of these are excuses for why we don't want to choose love.

The concept of love has been hijacked in our culture. Love is now a runaway train, off the tracks and speeding toward a cliff full of passion, fury, emotion, and nothing sustainable. Love is not presented or done, for the most part, God's way, and thus, love comes and goes with the seasons. But God's love never changes because he chooses love and He chooses us. God's love is constant. And isn't that what we really want? Someone who will love us on our best and worst days? Someone who will be constantly smiling upon us, encouraging us, forgiving us, extending their hand to us?

If one does not resolve to grow in love, then one will likely be horrible at covenant. Our culture makes it all too easy to justify the two lines growing apart, and each party has their reasons for why that growing together thing was just impossible and why they were absolutely justified in choosing option B. But meanwhile, we are dying for examples of those who have worked it out and have chosen love over the long haul.

So back to my big moment...

After getting clarity about the decision that was at hand, God led me to a fairly obscure story in the Bible about David and his relationship with Mephibasheth, Jonathan's son. David, out of his love for his good friend Jonathan, who had died, asked if there were any relatives of Jonathan's that he could bless. David found out that a son was left orphaned by Jonathan named Mephibasheth. David sent for him and he was found, lame and scared out of his mind thinking that David wanted to eliminate him because he had the blood of the former king. Instead, David welcomed him, offered him a place at his table, and gave him land.

After reading that story, God asked me if out of my love for my good friend, whether I could warmly extend love toward her family. In essence, could I choose the growing toward option instead of the growing apart option? I wrote out a little contract in my journal and literally signed on the dotted line. I made a decision to say "Yes!"

As my first act of growing together, I chose to go visit her mom at work. As I pulled into the parking lot, I heard God whisper, "That was the last thing I needed to do before you got pregnant." The next month, I was pregnant with Judah, our son. I guess covenantal love results in some choice fruit.

Ask the Holy Spirit to show you more about covenant. Look up the covenants He's made in scripture. What do you see about his character?

*As this book is in first print, it is now six years after my initial decision to covenant with Dawn's family in this special way. Let me tell you, they have blessed our lives in immeasurable ways. They are grandparents and parents to our family. They are champions for us. They are our support system here in Wichita. We have benefited more than I can even explain from this relationship with them. We are so grateful for them!

3.2

Home-inspired culture reflects God's heart through us and to us.

This evening I oversaw the bedtime routine for Judah. We were having a great time playing and then came the time to clean up and have a bath. We have foam letters in our bathtub and Judah loves holding up a letter and telling me what it is. Recently, I've been asking him, "What sound does that letter make?" So tonight, he held up "S" and I asked him what sound it makes. He said, "sss, sss." It's just fun.

Sometimes because the sounds are a new thing he's learning, he will give the completely wrong sound. Like today he held up "L," and I asked him what sound it makes. He said, "fff, fff." I corrected him and told him, "No. 'L' sounds like 'llll' as in 'letter' or 'love.'" We moved on. I asked him about "M." What letter was it? What sound does it make? He again was completely off, so I told him "M" makes a sound like "mmm" as in "mama." And without even missing a beat, Judah looked me in the eyes and said in a very tender voice, "Love mama."

Oh my goodness! My heart melted. I felt so filled up, so seen, so valued from those two little words. It was a sweet moment. And I started thinking about why it was so sweet. I think it was so sweet because I've done so many things over the course of his short two and a half years that have gone unnoticed. Even before he was born, I was sacrificially giving to him as I contended, prayed, and chose a lifestyle that would best set him up for a good life. And then when he was born, it was another level of laid down love as I got up with him, nursed him, held him as he cried, and changed more diapers than I could ever get my head around. Most recently, we've been going through waves of boundaries being tested, fits, and willful rejection.

And all the while, I am contending for him, choosing him, choosing to love him day after day.

In that moment tonight, sitting on the bathroom floor, something clicked for me about God. See, I've never really bought all the verses in scripture about His response to our worship. It's been just pretty over the top for me. Especially verses in Song of Solomon about how we as the bride of Christ have ravished his heart, just one glance of our eyes and we have ravished his heart. For me, a lot of those verses have sounded nice, but wow, so dramatic. I mean, I've always thought, I worship Him because He is worthy, He is Lord, He is King, He is good. I worship Him because it's the right thing to do. And all of this is true, but I don't think I've ever become fully convinced about how He feels when I worship Him until tonight.

God laid the groundwork for loving us way more extravagantly than I did with Judah. Before the foundation of the world, He knew us. He then saw us trapped in the inferior curse of Adam, so He sent His Son to put Him on display, die a brutal death and rise again so that we could be transformed by His love. He then sent His Holy Spirit to apply the work of redemption to people's lives in time and space. Millennia passed and one day I was born, someone He had known since before the foundation of the world, someone He had already died for, someone He had already made provision for. And I grew up not knowing of His love or His kindness. I grew up never hearing about Him. I grew up without acknowledging Him.

Then, over the course of a season in college, I came to know Him, and I finally recognized it was Him and His love and I finally said, "I love You."

I get it. For a dad who has laid down His life and put His best on the line for the ones He loves, to have them say in time and space, "I love you," means the world! It fills His heart in a way that I can only taste in a small way as I hear my son say the same.

Ask the Holy Spirit to show you how God's heart was revealed to you and through you recently.

3.3

Home-inspired culture encourages maturation not perfection and emphasizes relationship above productivity.

We just moved into a house with three mature trees out front. As fall rolled in and the leaves started to turn, these long pods began to fall from the tallest tree. The pods turned into a full-time clean-up operation for the last few weeks as they start to gather on the ground in the hundreds. My husband is usually the one who does this work, but yesterday I decided to help a brother out, so I marched out there with Judah to clean them up ourselves.

As I was gathering them together in piles, Judah was mostly playing with his miniature tractor, his t-ball tee, and his bat. He had little to no interest in the pods. But when he started to realize that they were in piles which could be trounced on, he started to perk up. He first engaged by standing on a pile and scattering several of the pods I'd just gathered. I won't lie, my anxiety level was rising. That kind of work isn't really the most fun thing for me anyway, and then to have someone actually working against the end goal... ugh.

Lucky for me, I was at least aware of the anxiety. I realized that compared to the hundreds of pods I could gather in a single sweep, Judah could only scatter a few. This calmed me down. I started talking to God about the whole thing. I asked God something like, "God is this how you remain calm when there are professing believers working counter to your mission for the world? You are so much more powerful than your children. And you see all that is happening all around to gather. Those who scatter a bit here and there can't stop the job from getting done."

After my initial anxiety, I adjusted Judah's focus a bit and asked if he would come near the trash can and throw the pods in the can. He was happy to do that as the can then became the largest form of a basketball hoop he'd ever seen. After a short while, he was merrily grabbing pods and throwing them up into the bin. He was participating with me in the gathering process. I then saw something else... it was such a joy for us to be working together on the same goal toward the same end. I so enjoyed just working together with him. No matter that he hardly made any dent in the work that had to be done. For me it was the working together that thrilled my heart.

I thought about God again. Typically, I've thought that when I'm attempting something for God that, even though there were some good things about it, there were lots of missing pieces, lots of things lacking, lots of shortcomings. But there in that moment with Judah I saw something different. Were there shortcomings to what he was doing? Yes. Namely that he picked up less than one percent of the pods. However, those were covered by my love for him, my conscious awareness of his limitations (namely that he was two) and his joy in doing the work with me.

Is that how God sees me? I'm beginning to think yes. God enjoys my feeble efforts to help Him in His mission. He enjoys the serving together. He enjoys the co-laboring. And although He sees all my shortcomings and mistakes, His love covers me over and over again.

Ask the Holy Spirit if you value maturation over perfection. Ask Him if you prioritize relationship above productivity.

3.4

Home-inspired culture is built on small practical acts done in love.

When I was in high school back in the '90s, homemaking courses like cooking and sewing were offered under the banner of home economics. Back then, although it was kind of fun to learn how to cook simple meals like spaghetti and learn how to make a pillow, we poked fun at the classes calling them irrelevant and outdated. After all, it was getting so that one could buy a really nice pillow more cheaply than making one, and homemade meals were becoming a thing of the past. After all, most women were not stuck at home anymore. They were out in the workforce, running companies, leading whole NGOs, kicking butt and taking names. It wasn't soon after my high school days that those classes were taken out of my high school curriculum.

At the age of 35, I had my first child. In my 20s, I had developed some of the skills those home ec teachers tried to impart. I learned to cook using real vegetables and meat. I learned how to manage a kitchen and how to keep household systems running pretty smoothly. But I had no appreciation or vision for most of that work, save cooking healthy meals.

This stemmed from a long history of women in my family who had mixed feelings about the more domestic affairs. And let me tell you, I can understand why. My paternal grandmother had a real drive and conviction that she wanted to change the world and yet she felt stuck in the home. She was served up cultural examples of ideal women like in the show *Leave it to Beaver* where Barbara Billingsly played an always put together, always smiling, always wholesome mom whose house was always perfectly manicured. My grandma knew that there was real pain in the world. She wanted to solve real problems. She wanted to be strong. She wanted to enter into the grit of life and be in the thick of the mess. She wanted to really change something. She saw women like Barbara Billingsly's character as missing the boat.

My mom was a young woman as the third wave feminist movement was under way. She became a professional musician right in the middle of huge cultural shifts as women explored territory beyond social norms. She had mixed feelings about becoming a mother and often felt pulled in many directions as she navigated a full-time job and family life. She amazingly always managed to juggle both home and work, but she was too busy to really impart the power of home to me.

I believe that the feminist movement was a reaction to the prescriptive boxes put on women by culture. There were definitely boxes. In the 1950s in America, it was the cultural trend for women to stay home, even if they had very little to do. It was culturally understood that women were to be in the home. So much potential for women was lost, and many dreams were killed because of prescriptive boxes. My grandmother and mother saw the religious confines of these boxes and did not want to live within them.

The feminist movement did a lot of good for women in terms of breaking us out of those boxes. But in my opinion, it also injected some pretty horrible lies about women into our culture. Those lies had to do with the idea that our potential would only be realized "out there," outside of the home, in the workplace where the "real" work is done. That movement agreed with some fallacies about the power and potential of home because if we were to compete and keep up, we were to be breadwinners as well. There's nothing wrong with earning a fair wage, but our potential to change the world can never be reduced to how much money we make.

I think that culturally this led women who were wives and moms in the '60s and '70s to generally see the home as a means to an end. I think women started to see home as a stopping place, a place to eat and sleep. I think the world-changing potential of consciously and intentionally building a Kingdom culture at home was lost far and wide on a generation.

But me, I'm starting to see that there is a world beyond the wardrobe. If I just peer a little deeper, I'm starting to see that home ec was actually an attempt to whet my taste buds for something so potent and so significant that it may in fact be one of the most important things I ever do.

No one is telling me I have to stay at home, thanks to a lot of the work that women like my mom did to expand our possibilities. But now I'm making the choice to prioritize home. I'm not throwing away my personal potential. I'm choosing to put it on the back burner in order to have home making on the front burner. I tell people that right now with little kids, I spend about five to ten percent of my time on personal calling by choice. It won't always be this way. My mom taught me that I, as an individual, have something very valuable to contribute to this world, and I'm so grateful for that inheritance. At the same time, she sees the joy and the richness that I have as I nurture and cultivate my family. And as I delve into the riches of home, I see a world of potential through tiny acts of practical love done day in and day out.

Ask the Holy Spirit for vision to see the small, practical acts of love in your Home Inspired.

3.5

Home-inspired culture teaches each member to honor all people.

Recently, I was at a playground with my two-year-old son. As he was attempting to get water from the water fountain, an older mom and her seven-year-old daughter came to play as well. The mom was friendly enough. We chatted a bit about the weather. It seemed that her daughter had a vivid imagination. She told her mom she wanted to play restaurant and her mom was to be the waitress. But as I encountered this mother and daughter in bits and pieces, I saw that something significant was out of order. In each of the games, the daughter was in charge and the mother was willingly her servant. In another game, the daughter climbed to a high place and told her mother in a bold way, "I am the queen. You are my servant. Now fetch me some water!"

Okay, so I may have read too much into the situation. After all, this was just pretend, right? But then I watched as this girl came down the slide right on the heels of my little son. She was being sweet, but it was a little too close for comfort. Her mother gently said something to her, but she dismissed her mother's input and justified her actions.

My intention is not to criticize this mom. But it got me thinking. The first commandment in the Ten Commandments given in Exodus about human interaction has to do with honor. It says, "Honor your father and mother." Honoring father and mother should have nothing to do with a rigid authoritarian structure. It has everything to do with trust and love. Children must learn honor if they are to function properly and are to live as they were created to live.

A culture of honor is essential to home inspired. This first starts with mom and dad's relationship with God. If humility and honor is not established there, then it won't be anywhere else in any depth. We as humans have this funny decision to make: are we "lord" of our lives or is the God of the universe Lord? When we make a decision to make God the Lord, it begins a process of learning to honor the one to whom we've pledged allegiance. He gives us the grace and empowers us to live that way. But we get to surrender and honor Him, and as we do, we learn about honor.

Once mom and dad learn to honor God, they must then learn to honor each other. Easier said than done, right?

Yes, but essential. It is essential that we put honor on display in and through broken, fleshy vessels because the world is waiting for this: covenant that honors, not just tolerates. The world is waiting for covenant that celebrates one another's differences instead of mocking them.

This culture of honor in marriage is fought for each day. It forces us to weed out our acquired beliefs about the opposite sex and about our specific mates. It forces us to use our words, our actions, and our attitudes to treat our spouse as valuable, powerful, important, and worthy of respect. It forces us to own and work through hurt in our hearts that's come through the course of marriage—bitterness never breeds honor and connection, it breeds justification for my position and for why the other should be condemned. It is a choice, a daily choice, to do these things so that we can put the culture of honor within our marriages on display to our children and those who enter our homes.

A culture of honor requires us to honor our children and also to expect them to honor us. This means that they may not hit us when they are disappointed with a decision. They may not speak to us in disrespectful ways. If they want to do that, they need to go somewhere, calm down, and then come back to have a conversation. It means that we choose to build trust and love with them even when it is tough and that they choose trust and love even when it is tough because whether they like it or not, they have been given parents by God. It's one of those things that they didn't choose. So by choosing to honor their parents, as imperfect as they are, they are actually choosing to honor God, and God will reward them.

Honor must be established because honor INSISTS on treating the members of the family as they really are: created in God's image and therefore of immense intrinsic value.

This mom at the playground was doing her best. But I believe she was doing herself and her daughter a great disservice by allowing her daughter to dishonor her. It will steal from the peace, prosperity, and potential fruitfulness of their home.

Ask the Holy Spirit how you can cultivate honor in your home.

3.6

Home-inspired culture prioritizes living before the face of God.

My son and I like to read before nap time. Recently, I've come upon this gem of a book by Max Lucado called *You Are Special*. It's about a little world of wooden people called Wemmicks. They are all made by Eli the woodworker, and they preoccupy themselves by going around and giving stars and dots to one another. They give stars if something is well done or someone is very talented. They give dots if someone doesn't hit the expected mark.

The main character, Punchinello, finds himself unable to get any stars. He only gets dots as he tries harder and harder to live up to the standards the others set before him. Then he meets a girl who has no stars or dots. Even when people try to place them on her, they don't stick. She told him to go see Eli the woodworker. So, he goes. There, at Eli's workshop, he is met with love and compassion and a totally different way of seeing himself through Eli's eyes. Eli says, "You are special because you're mine."

I've been thinking about this little book and thinking about its message. It's so powerful. In this book, the author lays out two systems of identifying oneself. One system hangs on the praises or criticisms of others. The other hangs on the truth of the Maker Himself.

As I've meditated on this, I've thought about the decreasing value for character development in children. I know it sounds like a big leap, but let me take you there...

In our culture, we've tried to do away with absolute truth. By doing this, we also do away with a God who gives good, universal boundaries which we are to follow to be fully human. By doing this, we are essentially forsaking a lifestyle in which we refer to Him for our validation. We create our own standards for our lives and the lives around us. With the erosion of absolute truth, we have become man-centered in our morality, in our versions of God, and in our faith in humanity. The only absolute truth in this philosophy is that there is no absolute truth. It's the ultimate tyranny of the masses. We have subjected ourselves to the shifting standards of cultural opinion. These fallacies permeate our public school system, our media, and even some of our churches.

If there is no clear focus on living before the face of an unchanging God with unchanging expectations for people to live their best lives, then there is really no need for character development for kids. If this is the case then, what do we focus on as parents to ensure that our kids are growing in a healthy manner? We focus on milestones and brain development! Has little Johnny learned to swim? Has he learned to read at age 2.5? Has he played his first professional soccer game yet? Skills skills skills!! A star for you! A dot for you! We've got to train our children to be the best and perform the best. We put them on elite teams. We push them to practice more, to train harder, to run faster. I feel a pressure in this regard all the time in interactions with friends and family; the big question being, "Is my little son keeping up? Is he learning skills so that he can be all he is supposed to be?"

Meanwhile, true character development, training our children to do what is right before God, is left on the back burner.

So, what does it look like to value character development and ultimately value love in my house? It looks like me praising Judah's choice to tell the truth even more than his impressive ability to remember his letters because his truth telling preserves the connection he has with God and with his parents. It looks like me insisting that he practice honoring and, yes, obeying his mother and father. It looks like me helping him to make a choice to be grateful. It looks like me enforcing his good stewardship of his toys every night because these are the beginnings of a good relationship with creation. It looks like me modeling a worshipful life for him and encouraging him to enter into worship too. It looks like me revisiting a situation he refuses to forgive until he is willing in his heart to let that person off the hook and not remain angry or vengeful.

This will mean that Judah might not swim at age 0 like everyone else's kid. But I hope this means that Judah will have the character to know who he is living for and who he is choosing to love. He doesn't live to get stars and avoid dots from the other Wemmicks. Their good opinions and "love" will come and go. He is looking to Eli, his maker, who IS love and he is living under the eternal law of love to guide his choices and actions. I trust as he does this, he will model the missing love this world longs to see and he will be firmly planted in a never fading love relationship with his maker.

Ask the Holy Spirit to reveal to you your priorities as a parent.

Chapter 4

Home-Inspired Defense

While this could be a chapter about physical protection of a home, I choose to take a different approach. I choose to address some of the potential invasions of ideas into home inspired. Ideas are what create beliefs which create action patterns which create cultures. Ideas matter. And in this world of home inspired, we have to be very conscious of the ideas that are affecting our beliefs and our choices. These essays address some of the potential pitfalls in home inspired "thinking."

4.0

Home-inspired defense protects against the fear of man and seeks wisdom from God.

I've spent a lot of time lately writing about the home and about its incredible and intelligent design. I've spent a lot of time lately thinking about systems and ideological undercurrents that could potentially distort or undermine the power and possibility in this micro-nation. I believe those have been worthwhile lines of thinking. There is a trap, however. When I start to think that I have a corner on the market of doing home inspired, then I begin to justify my way of doing things as the right way. We go down the path of right vs. wrong, staying home vs. daycare, home schooling vs. public schooling, bottle feeding vs. breast feeding, and the lists, and the camps, and the justifications go on and on.

Bottom line: We all want to do right by our kids and we all want our kids to turn out well!

So, I started thinking a bit more about this comparison game and how it's just not the real issue. The issue is boiled down to **wisdom**: godly, often simple, sometimes complex wisdom.

The Bible says, "The fear of the Lord is the beginning of wisdom." And, "... Above all get wisdom!"

I started asking myself, "Why do I feel some anxiety when I talk to certain friends about their parental choices while I feel no anxiety talking to other friends who are actually making the same exact choices?"

The answer: It's not the choices or the actions themselves that are the issue. It's the driving force behind the choices. It's the motive behind the choice. The motive boils down to what we want. And I want to see moms be driven by or motivated by no other force than wisdom. Wisdom is God's word and God's way applied to one's situation whatever it may be. When choices in any area of life are made with a foundation of wisdom, then they are informed and blessed by the grace of God. They are in the way of God.

James 1:5-8 says,

> And if anyone longs to be wise, ask God for wisdom and he will give it! He won't see your lack of wisdom as an opportunity to scold you over your failures but he will overwhelm your failures with his generous grace. Just make sure you ask empowered by confident faith without doubting that you will receive. For the ambivalent person believes one minute and doubts the next. Being undecided makes you become like the rough seas driven and tossed by the wind. You're up one minute and tossed down the next. When you are half-hearted and wavering it leaves you unstable. (The Passion Translation)

I have prayed for wisdom to parent my child in the way of the Lord and often those choices fly in the face of conventional ideas. I pray for wisdom for many others. It's the key thing. It's central to making decisions for your family that are the word of God applied and put into action.

And that is the nature of wisdom. The questions wisdom would ask are, "How do I apply God's nature and character, His way, to this situation?

How has God designed my family? And how can I line up my actions, choices, and habits big and little to align with that design?"

Problem? It's not as simple as a "how to" article on Huffington Post. And it's not as simple as subscribing to the parenting way or philosophy that works so well for another friend. It might not work for you and your family.

So, how do we get wisdom? The fear of the Lord. It comes back to our commitment to honor God and His ways above all else. And this is motivated by a heart to see God glorified on the Earth. This is why James says that we must ask without wavering. Are we willing to commit to doing what God wants us to do for our family, even if it looks strange or falls out of the norm in our circles? It comes back to soberly and intentionally understanding His ways and His character so that decisions can be made more and more wisely.

What are some impediments to wisdom?

The fear of man: If you can't stand the opinions, get out of the kitchen. Ha! People will always have opinions about how you are raising your kids. You cannot be swayed to and fro by the opinions of friends, family, or even your most well-intentioned Christians. Those will change as the waves on the sea. God's wisdom will steady your boat and give you clarity.

"Keeping up with the Joneses" or the comparison game: If this motivates you—having the next best X, Y, or Z, the most talented son or daughter, or the best behaved child, in other words, winning the comparison game—then you will lose. If it becomes a competition or a comparison game for you, then you lose and so does your child. It makes what is wise for your particular family and child cloudy and unimportant.

Religious pressure: Yes, even within the church, we can get to be "know-it-alls." Even though we have a big and extremely diverse and endless God, we can get locked down into thinking that we know the right way to raise children. And we can believe the lie that if we just do it like those in X religion do it, our kids will be great. Sadly, we cannot rest on the example of those who've gone before us to navigate the very real and multifaceted problems we face in parental decision making in 2018 and beyond. We must rely on the Holy Spirit.

So, what motivates you and your decisions when it comes to your family? Is it the fear of man and its many different forms? Or is it the fear of the Lord? If you've learned how to fear the Lord, you are on track to a life filled with wisdom for you and your family!

Ask the Holy Spirit to clarify what motivates you. Ask Him for wisdom about specific situations where you know you are tempted to fear man.

4.1

Home-inspired defense protects hope.

It does not fail to amaze me the depths of perversion and evil to which some in our nation have stooped. The killer clowns craze is a good example of people who are enjoying agreement with the wicked one, personifying evil spirits and scaring little children and adults witless.

When I hear about some of the random acts of evil happening in our nation, I can quickly spiral downward. I want to batten down the hatches, and I want to protect my son above all else, as in, never let him outside again.

Tonight was one of those nights. After hearing stories about the killer clowns, something flipped in me. There is real evil out there and I need to protect my son. My thoughts came at rapid fire: *Where's the gun? How do I shoot it? I need to learn how to defend us because this is getting dark.*

As I was reeling downward and trying to get through the end of the day, I stepped into my kitchen and heard God's still voice say, "Naomi, there is hope."

Was this a hope issue? I didn't think so. But in a real way, YES, it is a hope issue. Here's the deal: As I closed all the curtains and tightened my grip on the few things over which I have control, I was thinking, "The world is very dark, the world is very evil. I need to desperately protect those I love and myself."

While I do think there is a defensive element to this battle, if I stay there, my world remains very small and I stop living out my life believing that God is alive and active outside the four walls of my home. This is a very dangerous mentality. It limits God and it limits the possibilities for my life as an agent of Kingdom expansion.

Sure, I can tell myself, "Well, my role in kingdom expansion is to raise a son and make a home." And while I think that is one of my central roles, am I excusing the fear that has engulfed me? Am I allowing it to hang around and become a regular guest at my dinner table? If so, this is absolutely not okay.

It is not okay for a child of the most High God to ever agree with fear.

It is not okay for a saint of Light to submit to darkness and to be so overwhelmed by the darkness that they forget that light dispels darkness with one flicker.

It is not okay for one who is filled with the power of the Holy Spirit to be overpowered by a force that they could annihilate with one small prayer.

We are so powerful, light-filled, and loved.

What if, despite the killer clowns, my life is teeming with possibility because I have a big God who loves to make a way where there seems to be no way. I serve a God who loves to take what seems like the darkest night and turn it around and make it day. I serve a God who does this over and over in accounts in the Bible and who does it over and over in the world today. What if this is completely a hope issue as the saints of God turn and prophesy a new day of light into the darkness?

I choose to believe that I am born again to a living HOPE: a hope that cannot and will not ever die. I am rich with hope because my hope is active and living. I've got the winning advantage because this commodity is scarce and so desperately needed in our day.

So, take your best shot, killer clowns—my God is bigger and faster. My Father has my back and brings me hope when I need it most.

Ask the Holy Spirit to help you protect hope in your home.

*I used a little program by Dr. Caroline Leaf called 21 Day Brain Detox to help consciously attack the presence of fear in my thinking. I think it's great if you see a particular toxic issue that you are repeatedly and habitually struggling with. http://21daybraindetox.com

4.2

Home-inspired defense understands the true nature of the battle.

Our soon to be two-year-old son Judah loves the story of David and Goliath. I'm not sure exactly what it is, but something about the action, the tension, the overwhelming odds stacked against the protagonist, and the surprising victory. It's a formula that works every time!

As he naps, I'm reflecting on the state of our nation. We now have the bathroom wars which we would never have considered ten years ago. This is a fight against basic biology. Now our gender is based on how we feel. In a real way, it's the ultimate rebellion against God, saying that we don't like what He gave us or how He chose to make us. It's like saying, "We choose to usurp God's role in our lives and make ourselves something else." It's ludicrous. But here we are. And in a real way, I feel like we are looking at Goliath peering down at us and laughing.

I don't know about you, but a lot of the time, I feel pretty intimidated, much like the Israelite army. A lot of us, me included, are good at hiding our heads in the sand and thinking that nothing will really hit us where we can feel it. We retreat into our comfort circles at home, in church, or on Facebook. But for those of us who want to start thinking about being the

"Davids" of our generation, it's hard to even know where to start. This is not a flesh-and-blood giant that can fall with one smooth stone.

We find ourselves in the snowballing effect of many ideas that have worked together to undermine everything that we know makes for a strong society. So, in this day and in this hour, what are OUR smooth stones? How can we fight this giant of biological confusion and rebellion in our nation with an alternative warfare that will catch Goliath off guard?

I'd like to submit, with total openness to other options, that we have five stones. They are covenant, love, prayer, family, and "cultivating our own gardens."

But before I go into each of these, let me just say, I really appreciate those who are battling on the lines of civil advocacy when it comes to the bathroom wars. I applaud anyone who will stand up and be brave against the tyranny of ideas that is wreaking havoc on our nation right now. It is, however, my conviction that there is a rotting away in the areas I'm about to describe that have made for the weakness and therefore vulnerability of our society.

So, let me describe these five smooth, seemingly innocuous, stones:

1. **Covenant**: A society is only as strong as its commitment to covenant. Our God is a covenantal God. We must understand that God covenants with us but also looks for a people who will be covenant keepers with Him. How does this look? It looks like a single-minded devotion, gratitude, and service to the One who bled and died for us. It looks like strong individuals who are ever growing in their abilities to be Spirit-governed because that's what covenant keeping is all about. It looks like every professing Christian

becoming willing to die for the sake of their covenant with God if necessary.

Once convictional covenant with God is established, we then emphasize covenants with each other. We hold our marriage vows as sacred and are careful about this union. We vow before God and others that we will do what it takes to keep our marriage together. Burn all bridges. Stick it out. And, just a tip for anyone who just got married, that means taking the option of divorce out of your really intense fights. Introducing this idea only bring instability and damage to your relationship; it is never to be used as a source of power or control.

2. **Love**: Our ideas of love are so perverse in our culture. This smooth stone of love goes right along with the idea of covenant. It is a choice. Say that with me: "LOVE IS A CHOICE." It is not a feeling, although feelings can complement it a lot. Love chooses to contend for a person's best, even to the lover's own hurt. Love suffers long. Love sacrifices. Love gives. Love pours out. And love does not passively stand by as the loved one makes choices that are the spiritual equivalent of ingesting cyanide. Love does not rejoice in being right, but rejoices in truth. Love only wants the truth to be acknowledged and honored. Love and truth cannot be separated.

We are called to love our neighbor. Who is that? Anyone who is in front of us. We are called to love our families, our neighbors, our friends, the school down the street, the college campus down the road. We are called to love people. Period. And when we resolve that we WILL love—as in, CHOOSE to love—we position ourselves in a very powerful place.

3. **Prayer**: Possibly the most undervalued weapon we have is humbling ourselves and invoking the power and the activity of a God who is wonderful, sovereign, loving, and good. And this means talking to Him, depending on Him. That's right. Better than reading all those self-help books, get to know the Holy Spirit who gives wisdom. Pray. And listen. Listen and pray. It does wonders for your life and mine. It also has the added benefit of turning our attention to what God IS doing instead of what He seems to not be doing at any given moment.

4. **Family**: There is nothing as powerful as a strong family in terms of demonstrating love to a watching world. It is the best and most intensive discipleship program ever known to man. God designed it that way. Marriage is such a beautiful picture of unity and diversity wrapped in one. And the fruit of that is this beautiful blend of both individuals in the marriage: little eyes, little feet, little hands who need to be nurtured and trained, guarded and nourished, comforted and disciplined. If this is done well, my friends, nothing can stop us.

5. "**Cultivating our own gardens**": I know this is a long name for one smooth stone, but this stone is powerful and here is what it is. You have a space and a place in this world, "your land," so to speak. You live in some type of residence, have some network of relationships, have some neighbors, have some spaces around you. How are you cultivating love in the relationships around you? How

are you cultivating beauty in the space around you? How are you cultivating justice in the systems around you? You, yes you. You have a mini-kingdom to tend to and to cultivate. So get after it.

These, my friends are my five smooth stones. They won't defeat this Goliath in one day, but they are powerful! Hold them in your pocket. Meditate on them, treasure them no matter what. If you do, you will see the power of God with us as we go to battle.

Ask the Holy Spirit to give you clear focus and confidence in God's way when it comes to battle.

Chapter 5

Home-Inspired Economy

During His time on Earth, Jesus talked about money a lot, so I thought we should chat about it as well. This aspect of home inspired fascinates me. Home-inspired economy involves wisdom, tension, discernment, faith, and growth in many areas. Most of us inherited a dysfunctional "norm" in our relationship with money. It is my belief that if we inherited any type of fear or anxiety in our relationship with finances, we have also inherited the various ways in which we can idolize it. On the flip side, when we inherit wisdom and peace with money, we can use money to bring glory to God in all kinds of ways.

It's all about a journey with the Holy Spirit when it comes to finances. He is continually teaching us about His ways in this area and how to trust Him while taking personal responsibility for our choices and lifestyle.

It's my opinion that He calls us to different journeys in this area because our callings require different relationships with it. I hope that these glimpses into our journey will bless you in your own.

5.0

Home-inspired economy reflects the values and priorities of heaven.

My husband and I just learned to make and keep a budget. I know what you might be thinking: "She's 37 and she's finally learning how to make a balanced personal budget?" Yes, and let me say, what a revelation! I remember learning about this form of stewardship back in my 20s, but I never really applied it until we got married and I saw more of the need to at least track our expenses. So, for several years, I would track and then would hope to at least have a zero total balance at the end of the month. But only in the last few months did we learn how to plan and direct our spending, giving, and saving. This has "afforded" (cheesy pun for free) us new levels in growth with some great boundaries on our spending, some good momentum in our savings, and some conscious, intentional giving.

It's been so good! And what I've learned is that a piece of God's heart is reflected in solid, transparent money management. The idea that God is a just God, that God cares about just weights and measures, says a lot about Him as an accountant. In a real way, God crosses every "T" and dots every "I." The little things of dollars and even cents do not evade Him. He is a detail-oriented God. And it honors Him when we are honest about our budget, when we account for where our income goes, and when we make clear decisions about how we direct our resources. There is something just and right and true about it.

But in the same season, someone came into our lives and this relationship messed with my perfectly balanced budget....

Daniel is from Nepal. He came to the US with a visa to study, and then he fully planned to go and work illegally in order to send money back home to his widowed mom. After a few months in the US, Daniel had an encounter with God, and God convicted him about working illegally in the states. So, Daniel chose to trust God to provide, even though he was in a foreign land and had no means of providing for himself. Daniel began to see miracle after miracle of provision in his life, and then he started to develop a love for the people of his nation. He got his license and began to borrow our truck quite often to take other Nepali students to Walmart, host dinners for them, and love and bless them in any way he could.

We have been honored to walk with Daniel through this incredible transformation and to behold his breathtaking trust in God. After a while, we started to desire to give our truck to Daniel. But that wasn't just as simple as giving a truck away; it required raising funds for his gas, paying for his insurance, tags, and fees, making sure the truck was in good working order, etc.

After we had given the truck away, I looked at my previously beautifully balanced budget. It was a mess! We had hardly saved anything. We had to pour most of what we'd saved during our stringent budget-following months into the truck repairs and the insurance for Daniel. And to be quite honest, I was discouraged. I felt that it was the right thing to do, to give the truck to Daniel, and yet I felt that we were back to square one with our budget.

In this discouraged state, I turned to the Lord. The Lord led me to Proverbs 19:17: "Whoever is kind to the poor lends to the LORD, and he will reward them for what they have done."

This language is the language of dollars and cents yet brings an unlimited God into the budget. This blew my self-contained budget understanding out of the water! What if God partners with us in our budget? What if our family budget includes God? And what if it could not only reflect his justice but also reflect his mercy? What if we can rest on His promise that He sees our generosity to the poor and what if we really believed that He will not ignore that act of kindness, whether it be rewarded in this life or the next?

What a different concept of budgeting! What if a budget could reflect justice with all of its fairness, an eye for an eye and a tooth for a tooth, a dollar in for a dollar out? But what if a budget could be opened to often being overridden by the mercy of God?

What if mercy triumphs over judgement? What if that is what got me right with God in the first place? And what if it is my joy for my finances to reflect that heart of God for others?

While this may not mean the constant upward momentum of savings that I'd hoped for, this becomes about something bigger than me having a large nest egg. This becomes about me reflecting the heart of God for people, even in the most mundane area of our lives. This becomes about us as a family becoming a living Gospel, a living epistle reflecting the heart of God who sees the poor and disenfranchised. By us seeing them like He does and by having our pocket books reflect His heart of mercy toward them, we partner with Him in our budget and we can only be blessed by that!

Ask the Holy Spirit how your home economy can more thoroughly reflect the values of heaven.

5.1

Home-inspired economy protects against the love of money.

It's the love of money that is the root of all evil.
1 Timothy 6:10

I remember several years ago walking into the house of a business executive in our church. Everything was perfectly manicured, beautiful, and HUGE. At the time, I was reading a lot about caring for the poor and about the love of money. I'll be the first to say, I judged the heck out of this couple and their family. In my head, I was disgusted by their lifestyle, thinking that they were driven by the evil love of money which holds the weak down and blesses only a few. I was humbled to really get to know this family and see their heart for God. They were blessed with an abundance of resources and soberly took on this responsibility before the face of God.

It's easy to accuse the millionaire who is supposedly only looking to make his/her next million as being driven by the love of money. But what if that millionaire has the grace to make a lot of money and to give a lot of money away for the good of the culture, the society, and the Kingdom of God? Have they then fallen prey to the love of money? That's between them and God. But it's quite possible that the answer is no.

What about the frugal homemaker who lives on a tight budget and faithfully clips coupons? Surely, she hasn't fallen prey to this insidious spirit, right? Don't be so sure. We can, in our culture, become such professional bargain shoppers, professional consumers, that we too become obsessed with the love of money, saving money, keeping money, and building up the apparent security of money. It's the same thing as the lust-filled millionaire, just another side of the coin.

Or what about the man who never has enough? He doesn't have enough to adequately feed, clothe, or house himself or his family. Surely, he hasn't fallen for the love of money, he has little to none. Don't be so sure... it's quite possible that he thinks, "If only I had money, my life would be great! Money would solve all my problems." He too has fallen for the love of money.

So, if this sickness can infect the rich, the middle class, and the poor, how can we discern whether or not we have fallen prey to this sneaky trap?

Jesus provides a very clear way for us to tell if we have allowed the love of money into our thinking or decision making. In Matthew 6:25, it says, "Therefore I tell you, do not worry about your life, what you will eat or drink." The distinguishing feature in all of these scenarios is worry. The presence of worry is the indicator of the love of money. If we had a worry-ometer on our hearts, the higher it got, the more we would know that we have fallen into the evil love of money instead of loving and freely following God. Worry is rooted in fear. Fear is the antithesis of faithful trust in God. Worry sees the world and circumstances without a good and caring Father God in our lives and responds to that version of the world accordingly.

If we worry about financial provision constantly, then we are probably seeing our relationships in regard to their monetary value. Even if we mask it well, we can see the millionaire as someone who can invest in our new business venture, or the friend in need as a drain on our finances. If we aren't seeing relationships in this way, we could be making moves to control our spending, increase our saving, decrease our risk taking and increase our financial security. In contrast, we are making moves to gamble the little we have in order to increase our assets. In every case, the fear of losing everything haunts us and drives many of our decisions. Where is our trust? It's actually, if we are honest, in money. We think if we just had more, if we just had enough, if we just had a bigger savings or a bigger budget, then we would feel more secure or more peaceful, more powerful, more important. But our trust is sadly misplaced when we think more money will do these things for us.

It's also easy to think, "So what if I worry about money? That's my personal thing. It doesn't negatively affect anyone else. I'm not really hurting others by worrying about money, right?" Not right. This trap contributes to all kinds of evil. It creates a lack of compassion for the poor because they have nothing to offer us monetarily. It can also easily create a victim mentality in us where we always believe we are getting the short end of the stick when it comes to money. If we are victims, then it's very difficult to have compassion for anyone else. After all, we perceive that we are always lacking. This trap creates a lack of value for children because children are dependents and do not produce wealth. This trap creates whole systems that separate out social classes and justify this classism. This trap creates whole systems that serve people in their pursuit of money. And this trap creates oppressive ghettos for those who are left out of the "haves" camps. Just think about this: When you are worried about money, are you willing to give sacrificially? Are you willing to empower the least of these? Are you willing to look outside of yourself and help someone who isn't in the "haves" category? No. We close up, put our heads down, work hard, and work to get ours.

Recently, my husband and I learned how to actually do a real budget. And let me tell you, I became almost obsessive about it. We'd reduced our food budget significantly so that we could increase our savings, and that was good except that I was getting tighter and tighter about things. Meanwhile, I sensed the Holy Spirit asking me, "Naomi, why are you looking at your bank account so much?" It's His kindness that leads us to repentance. His questions brought me to this place of thinking about the love of money. We can judge others and think that they have fallen prey to the love of money, but maybe Jesus was talking about the normal man or woman who hasn't built up their immunity toward this insidious disease.

Jesus wants us to be free. He is holding out the keys to freedom from fear and from worry, we only need to take them and use them. Jesus wants us to be whole. Jesus wants us to operate with an awareness of and a total reliance on our inherited birthright as God's children. This means that the resources of heaven are opened to us. Jesus wants our spiritual and mental immunity to be strong enough to ward off the love of money and to run with Him as we use our resources to advance His Kingdom and trust Him to meet our needs.

Ask the Holy Spirit if you need to be freed up from the love of money. Ask Him to help you understand where the anxiety comes from. Forgive those who may have been involved in that injury. Repent for believing lies. Ask Holy Spirit to show you the truth.

5.2

Home-inspired economy seeks to reflect the multi-facets of God.

Imagine a large tent being raised up. The stakes have to go down solidly into the ground and then the center is pushed up. A tent can only work if there is tension between those stakes and that center post. If one of those stakes is loose, the whole thing collapses. When I think about home-inspired economy, it's not about just one thing. It's about the delicate tension between many things.

The tension I've felt lately has been between peaceful and intentional saving and thrifty spending while maintaining faith. Of course, there are other aspects to home economy such as investments and giving. But the former qualities are the ones I've most recently wrestled with.

Our life involves lots of people coming for dinner, staying at our home, etc., and that lifestyle costs money. Some of the money comes from the ministry, but a lot of it comes from our personal budget. This drives my personal food budget through the roof, often exceeding $1,000.00 per month.

Recently, I told my husband that in order to gain financial momentum, we needed to start saving at least ten percent of our monthly income. Given our lifestyle of serving people, this is challenging.

So, this entire month, especially at the end of the month, I've been working through the budget holding my breath. Is this going to work out? Are we going to be able to save ten percent? I'm working to drive my saving and frugal spending stakes into the ground.

At the same time, God has been showing me that He has promises for those who choose to seek FIRST His kingdom and righteousness. Matthew 6:33 says, "But seek first His kingdom and His righteousness, and all these things will be added to you." I don't think that this verse begins and ends with the idea of money. And I certainly don't think this concept begins and ends with tithing. I think, especially after this month, it is a daily choice. What's our financial priority at the end of the day? What is the dominant thought in our finances? And can we trust Him with the rest? Can we do our due diligence to be frugal and yet not rely only on our own devices to "get the job done" with our finances? I'm working to drive the center post of the tent up toward the sky. I'm working not to lose the perspective and the overall driving force for our desire for increase. The cry of our hearts has been, "Lord, increase our territory so that YOU will get the reward YOU deserve." At the end of the day, it's all about Him.

The tension is in careful stewardship as we keep in mind that the grace to prosper does not come from our stewardship but from His blessing.

To that end, here are a few very practical things that I've found that have helped us in that tension.

1. If I take cash out for the big budget variables like food, I am much, MUCH more careful with my spending.

2. I need to be diligent to balance the budget and yet also JUST as diligent to declare truth that I am partnering with a limitless God! My finances are not limited to this budget's restrictions.

3. I need to keep my peace no matter what. I need to know that it is going to be okay. If we have a big unexpected expense, it's going to be okay because God is on our side and it's His will to bless us.

4. I need to have a big picture mentality while still stewarding the details. If we don't save ten percent despite our best efforts, but we do save nine percent, that is a really huge improvement from what was happening in previous months.

5. I need to choose to rely on the solid promise of God that if we choose each day to seek first the Kingdom of God and His righteousness in our micro-economy that all these things will be added to us. It's a daily choice and often a very conscious battle and then resolution.

The tension continues. There is tension in wisdom. There is beauty in tension. We hope and pray that He will expand our tent pegs and that we will be able to give Him more glory with our lives. As we continue to walk in the tension within our micro-economy, I believe our reach will expand in four directions, cultivating stability and true abundance.

For us, the journey continues, as I'm sure it does with you. We are always tweaking and revisiting this topic, mostly reminding ourselves of the truths we already think we know. He is a great provider. He is trustworthy.

He calls us to be good stewards of His resources. He refines our hearts as we sojourn closer to His.

Ask the Holy Spirit which of God's "faces" He is wanting you to better understand when it comes to handling money. How does that play out in your day-to-day handling of resources?

Chapter 6

Home-Inspired Government

Oh, man, this one. All I can say is that there is this huge spectrum of truth in this arena. Sometimes, He requires us to really know that we are the God-given authority in the home and to establish the God-given order in the home. Other times, He asks us to focus on His heart to empower the ones we lead. It all comes back to relationship and to true, Godly order saturated with meekness.

6.0

Home-inspired government encourages obedience because obedience opens doors.

The complexities of having a near-three-year-old boy are hitting me. He is strong. He knows it. He has a will. He knows it. Also, he is fast! He can run faster than me a lot of the time. Time to hit the gym! Haha!

So, when it comes to leading him into truth and into righteousness, we've seen our struggles as of late.

Sometimes, he simply wants to say "No!" because he can. Other times, he doesn't like the limitations I put on him. Other times, he wants to do what he wants and he doesn't want me to change the direction of his will.

I can easily think to myself, "I want to honor his will and allow him to make his own choices." And I do want to honor his will, which might mean changing my own will. However, there is this place for him learning to simply obey his mom, partially because, as he obeys, worlds open up for him.

For example, right now we are working on obeying mom and being kind and gentle with our hands instead of trying to pick a "bar fight" with every little boy on the playground. I was thinking about this... what worlds open up for Judah if he obeys? He learns how to connect with people in a productive way. He learns how to play in a way that actually keeps friends instead of ostracizing them. He learns how to honor people's bodies and space and how to have self-control in peer relationships!

This is the power of obedience and of honor. As he honors me and trusts me, he obeys, and as he obeys, new worlds open up to him and he discovers higher ways of living.

Recently, I've had a similar experience with God. This may sound strange to many, especially to Americans, but I've had this feeling, this voice in my heart telling me to dance for God. I was a dancer in my "former" life and there is something about me and the way I am created that expresses who I really am through dance. But because of my own insecurities, I kind of thought dance was just too out there for the dignified worshipper. Nevertheless, it did not change the Voice. This Voice would say, "Dance for Me." It would follow me and I would rationalize it away. Then I would get away to some kind of conference and have random people tell me to dance for God. He wouldn't leave. He didn't relent.

My husband and I recently changed cities and churches. In our new church, there is a high value for following that Voice and a high value for extravagant worship. So, I recently had a huge breakthrough with dance! I actually danced for Him in corporate worship! No shame, no hiding, no "just barely" moving my arms. I all-out danced during worship!

Since that experience, God has downloaded wisdom to me about how He participates with us in worship, how He comes, about the power of His manifest presence coming, about His love, and about His mercy, His grace, and who I am in all of that! All of this was unlocked in one act of obedience.

He desires obedience rather than sacrifice.

I get that now. I know I can run around and do lots of really cool religious things for God, and those are fine. But they don't even come close to one power-packed act of obedience! That one act of obedience unlocks intimacy, friendship, closeness, and therefore insight and understanding that was otherwise locked to me. It's like a door. And the key is obedience.

I was thinking about why this is true. I believe it's because obedience, in its very nature, is an act of trust. It comes out of the relationship. It says, "I don't understand why you would be asking me to do this or do it this way, but I TRUST YOU, and I know you have my best in mind, so I will do it."

God is a relational God, not desiring people to do lots of great things for Him but desiring honest trust in Him. He looks for our willingness to lay down our own way of getting something or doing something. He looks for our trust in Him to tell us how to do it in a way that unlocks the mysteries of the Kingdom to us.

Only thing is, I didn't know what I was missing...

Just like Judah.

He often doesn't know what he's missing when he fails to obey, and neither do we.

I can only encourage his obedience when he chooses it and frustrate his plans to disobey so that the doors of wisdom can be unlocked for him and also for me.

Ask the Holy Spirit what new level of obedience He is calling you into. Ask Him for the grace to obey.

6.1

Home-inspired government is intended to protect and empower. *

Recently, we tackled the ever-intimidating potty training transition with our two-year-old. And let me tell you, I've learned so much about freedom and control and micro-nation government!

Ramping up to it, my husband and I had a very honest conversation. I asked him how he thought our son was growing and developing. He said that he thought Judah was doing so well in many areas. Then I confessed my insecurity; I told him I felt like I wasn't very good at teaching Judah life skills like sleeping in a big boy bed and training him to go in the potty. For me, those transitions seemed like really inconvenient interruptions to our "norm." And I like having a "norm." I like having a balanced, working system that keeps us on a routine. I don't like that routine to be interrupted or to be knocked off course. To me, the big boy bed and potty training transitions seemed like just that: painful disruptions from our comfortable "norm."

But when it really came down to it, my heart was uglier than that. I could justify delaying all the transitions by saying that they would disrupt our norm. But finally, I admitted to my husband that I feared losing control. I feared losing control of Judah's location at night. I feared losing control over the waste disposal management in our house. I feared losing control!

After admitting this, I realized here was the decision before me: Judah was at a point where he was ready for a new level of freedom and responsibility and there was a grace period for me to give it to him. But if I missed that window and continued in my controlling ways, only resentment and frustration eventually leading to rebellion would result in his heart. And when I took a good look at that, I said, "I'm not going to live that way."

Then I thought about the ever-insidious controlling spirit. Is it possible that the structure and rules and expectations perpetuated by a system at one point could be good and the right level of freedom for a season? But could it be that when the person in that system gets to a certain level of maturity, leadership has a choice? Can they choose increased freedom or control? And if leadership chooses control, does it follow then that those under that system must either leave the system to get the desired level of freedom or they must force the system to relinquish control in order to move forward?

Jesus encountered this control in the Pharisees. He saw the oppressiveness of their man-made rules. He was/is a perpetrator of freedom. He knows we were born for freedom. He provided structure for the disciples, but it was always about them discovering the power they had to bring the Kingdom of God themselves. He was constantly pushing freedom and responsibility down.

We see this fight for freedom and control everywhere in our current culture. When it comes to women leaders in the church, there is, on a broad scale, immaturity amongst women who want to lead in the church because they've never been given the freedom to do so. As a result, this is a justification amongst many men to keep women from leading. Those who are mature enough to lead often either have to leave and start their own ministries or push against the glass ceiling of church leadership in order to make progress.

We see this in the way our humanistic government functions today. The intellectual and political elite conclude that because the people cannot handle freedom in their minds, the government must regulate, must restrict and create a structure that "helps" the people in order to keep the "norm" functional. The problem with institutionalized government control is that it's very difficult to dismantle and thus keeps people perpetually under its thumb and immature. OR it incites revolt and rebellion as those who are mature enough to know what is happening insist on having their power. Case in point, The Revolutionary War.

So, back to my micro-nation, home. I did some research on potty training. Turns out, there is this woman who is considered a potty training guru. She's helped train thousands of people. And here's her basic method: instant freedom upgrade. Have your child wake up one day and tell them they are a big boy or girl now, gather all the diapers and wipes and anything diaper related with them and throw it away as a sign that this is the NEW norm. Then spend the next several days INTENSIVELY training them about the new norm, not forcing them to do anything, but helping them to adjust to the new norm.

Wow, this "way" was totally counter-intuitive for me. I thought, "Couldn't there be a more gradual way to help him get used to going in the potty?" But as we executed this woman's method, I realized something. There is so much power in giving people a CLEAR promotion and a CLEAR and instant upgrade in responsibility before they know that they can handle it. With new freedom must come new responsibility, and if the freedom upgrade is carefully timed, most people are ready for the responsibility that comes! Along with that, there is power in insisting that this person with new freedom can do it, can manage their freedom in the face of mess-ups. There is power in this because this is what a culture of freedom and empowerment looks like.

Have you ever been given a job to do by a boss or leader and then had that leader micro-manage you, even though they said it was yours? How does that feel? Horrible, right? Why? Because the release of control and the dispensing of freedom is unclear. In many ways, it would be better for them to never give you that responsibility than to give it and then subtly subvert your freedom by taking power back. We were designed to walk in ever-increasing levels of freedom along with that responsibility.

BUT—and this is a big but—when someone is given new freedom, then there is a whole new system to learn. It's like getting a new operating system. For example, someone coming out of jail. In prison, they had been told when and where to do everything in their lives. That is a system that works for a while. And then they are let go on good behavior. They often have no idea what to do with that freedom and end up returning to lawlessness because the intensive training and grace isn't there. And many will say, "Well I knew he/she was going to do that." They were never given a true fighting chance.

When we threw away our diapers, we told Judah, "Tell us when you need to go pee pee or poo poo." We told him this knowing full well that he would not know how to do it at first. We cannot expect when there is a huge release of freedom that people will know what to do with it or how things work. Judah would start to pee on the ground and we would rush him to the potty and celebrate any pee that made it into the potty. He soon learned. "Oh wow, I get praise and an M&M if I potty in the toilet. If I don't, I don't get any of that." He caught on very quickly! He still has his slipups, but he is, for the most part, done transitioning to this new level of freedom. It is my pleasure to see him know that he is so capable of managing freedom. And it is also my pleasure to train him in the ways of a new level, even if it involves a mess for me to clean up for a while.

Ask the Holy Spirit for wisdom about how to lead in such a way that protects and empowers those you lead.

*The title partially came from author and speaker Bill Johnson.

6.2

Home-inspired government leaders are confident in their call.

It never fails to amaze me how much kids can push their parents' buttons. At times, I think my son is a professional button pusher. He studies me. He knows the things that make me react and he knows the things that make me OVER react. Over the last few weeks, I've felt like the control panel of Apollo 11, and my son, a well-trained astronaut or "rocket ship driver" as Judah would say.

Recently, he's been walking away when I'm asking him a question or he will simply not answer when I talk to him. He knows that this just gets to me. And when I get provoked, it becomes a "my way or the highway" type of scenario. To be honest, I hate how this feels in my heart. There's a reason love is not provoked. When I get provoked, then it's truly just about me exercising my power over him and controlling him instead of about connecting with him.

I started to pray and ask God what the real problem was. He said, "You have been hurt." It was hard for me to accept that I have allowed a three-and-a-half-year-old to hurt me. But it's real. Instead of being honest with my son and telling him how I feel, I've "hulked up" and overridden him in many ways simply to protect myself. I started to see that I need to be honest with him and tell him when he is hurting my heart. I need to appeal to him and let him know how that makes me feel instead of just making a power move.

But I realized that my provocation went deeper. By my son not listening, I felt disrespected in my role as an authority in the home. As a leader, it never feels great to be disrespected. But I realized that when my son did this, it evoked a deep insecurity. The insecurity is that I'm not fit to be an authority in this home. I remembered a young man who was coming up as a leader in our campus ministry years ago. He was insecure, and as a result, he felt he had to control those he was given authority over. Insecurity in leaders produces control.

I dug deeper. My insecurity came from my analysis of my performance. I thought, "I have too many faults, too many issues, and too many failures. This disqualifies me as an authority in the home." Without realizing it, I'd based my confidence as a mom on my performance. Hence, I had perfection for my standard. Anytime I fell short of perfection, I would condemn myself. Great set up for success... HA!!

Performance can never be the basis for any leader's authority. Of course, there are things leaders can do that disqualify them. But there is a wide range of what is acceptable before that becomes an issue. In general, performance-based qualification naturally leads to perfectionism which leads to legalism which in the end kills!

On the flip side, the opinions of others can never be the basis for a leader's authority either. Public opinion will come and go, but the leader who is swayed by such input will never really be stable.

The only safe place on which a leader can confidently hang his or her hat is on the calling of God. If God has called me, then I'm here and I've got his blessing and his grace to lead, regardless of how beautifully I perform on any given day and regardless of the opinions of the peanut gallery.

In the ministry, one needs a clarity of calling and a confidence of one's proper placement. It can sometimes be questionable whether one is called into the full-time ministry or not. But within the family, God's calling is unmistakable. He gives us these little babies, and we don't get to go to the store to pick them out, neither do they get to go to the parent bank and pick out parents. All of this choosing is done by only one designer: God. So, God calls us to be moms and dads. God calls us to raise the particular children he's given. Our confidence can and should be in the call of God.

I'd believed several layers of lies:

1. I can't allow my son to see how his actions hurt me.

2. I need to control him because he is under my authority and he needs to know who is boss.

3. My calling as a mom comes from either how well he is doing or how well I think I'm doing.

Boil it all down and you get some solid truth:

1. If I allow him to understand how his disrespect hurts me, I am more connected to him.

2. I cannot control him, even if I want to. The only one I can control is myself on a good day.

3. My calling as a mom comes from God and no one else. I can be confident and secure that I am called to be mom in this house, with these kids, and God will give me the grace to fulfill His call.

So, thank you, little button pusher. Well done. You are disciplining your mom into greater levels of freedom and truth.

There are so many more subtleties and caveats to this area of home inspired. We are learning to rule and to cultivate our "gardens." This takes skill and a lot of faith. God knows this and He knows that our homes are some of the best incubators for rulers there are. So give yourself to this process. It's a good one. And it's learning more of the art than the science of influence and leadership. If you are with Him in the journey, He will show you what's next.

Ask the Holy Spirit where your confidence in leading at home comes from.

Chapter 7

Home-Inspired Foreign Policy

It is my personal conviction that our homes can be some of the most powerful witnesses that the Kingdom of God is here. We do have to really consider our attitude and approach in proclaiming this message to a watching world. While we balance our time spent looking outward and prioritize our families, there is a boomerang benefit to living missionally as a family. Your kids catch a lifestyle approach to evangelism and the advancement of the Kingdom of God.

7.0

Home-inspired foreign policy chooses love over fear.

God has not given us a spirit of fear, but of power, love, and self-control.

2 Timothy 1:7

Have you ever wondered about this verse? Why is self-control in there? I don't initially think of the opposite of fear as being self-control; I think of the opposite of fear as faith in God. So why did God put that reference to self-control in there?

Recently, in light of the terrorism overseas and in our nation, I've battled some serious fear. My mind goes to the "what ifs." What if there is an intruder in our home, and Judah, our son, and I are the only people there? What would I do? What if I'm at our gym and there is a gunman and I need to get Judah from the daycare and get out of there while people are panicking and stampeding? These, I have to admit, are not good imaginings. But my gut, fleshy reaction is, I want to control. Without realizing it, I feel out of control and so I try to clamp down on whatever I think I can control. I want control over any and all people who are EVER around my child. I want a weapon as a means of controlling the situation. I want safety by any means necessary. Fear leads to grasping at external control.

Recently, I've had several conversations with women who battle this control thing in the context of their marriages. They fear serious financial issues, so they try to control their husband's spending through pushing and criticism. They fear he is not aware of aspects of his job performance that will lead to his termination, so they alert and push him to make changes. The connection between fear and control is obvious in these situations. Yet, I can also see in their lives a perceived powerlessness resulting in survival tactics. These women, along with myself, have missed the truth of the matter. We can't control others, nor can we control most external circumstances.

So, why is the above verse about self-control so interesting? I find it interesting that God reminds us that we have a spirit of SELF control in the midst of fearful situations. We can CHOOSE love and faith no matter what. We can reign over our minds and we can CHOOSE a different way. And really, that's the only way anything ever changes! The minute we choose to walk with self-control as opposed to grasping at external control, we are no longer in the grip of the fear. We are operating at a higher level and can shift the culture in a small or large way.

I was recently at the YMCA waterpark with Judah. News of the Orlando mass shooting filled the airwaves, and it was just discovered that the gunman had Muslim roots and claimed to be connected with ISIS, the Muslim extremist group that has been terrorizing the world. I saw a woman who did not fit in. While most of the women had the typical swim gear on, she was covered from head to toe in long sleeves and a head covering. It was a different kind of swimsuit for sure. I knew she was a conservative Muslim. There was no other reason she'd be wearing such attire.

My mind went through several different scenarios and motivations for why she was at the park. It's a public place with a lot of people to possibly harm. My initial reaction was to try to keep an eye on her, watch for any sudden moves, and keep my son as far away from her as possible. Then I realized what I was doing. I was operating in fear and preemptively trying to control her and her interactions with me. I felt very justified. I felt, in some ways, like I had no choice. But then something interrupted my thinking. "Why would I choose to live like this when Jesus laid down his life for me? I am secured with Him. Could I move in the opposite spirit?" So, overriding my instinctual protection program, I chose to introduce myself and my son to her. Turns out she was vacationing from Syria, the location of the most damaging civil war of our day. She was sweet, timid, and eight months pregnant. Immediately, the story changed and I realized that this woman was simply visiting her sister in the states and looking to make a good life for her and her child. My fear dissipated and my compassion kicked in. Immediately, this woman became less of a perceived threat. Immediately, I could see myself in her and could see my face in her face.

Afterwards, I had to think, "What kind of example do I want my kids to have?" I want them to see me walk in love despite what the media is saying. I want them to see me have compassion for others who look different than me. I want to model the ways of love instead of the ways of fear. This takes immense amounts of self-control.

What overcomes fear and the consequential desire to control others and our external circumstances? It's that good old spirit of self-control. Self-control wills us to trust God and to walk in love despite our flesh raging against us. Self-control leads our being to the God way and enables us to become powerful people in the midst of difficult, pressure-filled, even life-threatening circumstances. I love that God has not given us a spirit of fear but of power, love and, yes, self-control.

Ask the Holy Spirit to show you your attitude toward those outside of your home. Does fear or love drive this attitude?

7.1

Home-inspired foreign policy models persistent love.

As of late, my son and I have been reading the well-known children's book *Green Eggs and Ham* by Dr. Suess. Anyone who was a kid knows the book. It's a basic book about two creatures: one named Sam, and another that Sam is trying to influence. It starts with Sam's unwilling friend declaring that he does not like Sam. Then Sam asks, "Do you like green eggs and ham?" And the guy goes on to say that he does not like them in any context or in any situation.

Sam continues to ask, continues to search, continues to press. Finally, they reach a tipping point where Sam appeals to this guy and says (to paraphrase), "You say you don't like them, but have you ever tried them? Try them and you may like them."

And this guy, wanting to get Sam off his back, decides to try them. And... he LIKES them.

It's funny, this relationship. The first funny part is that Sam isn't liked in this relationship until the tasting. And yet, Sam continues to pursue his proposed "buddy." Another thing is that Sam is NOT trying to convince his friend that he does like green eggs and ham, he is trying to get him to the point of decision. And the guy seems to have made decision after decision against the eggs and ham having never tried them.

It makes me think so much about the Gospel.

I think I've taken a much less tenacious approach with many people about the Gospel in the years I've been a Christian. First off, if people have told me they don't like me, I've backed off significantly, mostly out of felt rejection. Second, if they've told me that they do not like the Gospel, I've backed away and given them some version of a friendship without really telling them more about my faith. "At least I told them about my faith once," I would say to myself. But what if they rejected Him without ever trying Him? What if they rejected the IDEA of Him without really tasting and seeing that HE IS GOOD? Then I could learn a thing or two from Sam.

Well-known author and speaker Bill Johnson says, "Power demands a decision." Paul made clear reference to this when he said that in First Corinthians 2:4. They preached the Gospel not in word only but in POWER. An encounter with the power of God gives people a moment to decide, to taste and see that He is good.

I would do better to become convinced that people need to taste and see that God is good. I would do better to tenaciously pursue them with that truth. And I would do better to challenge them to taste Him for themselves and see for themselves.

Thanks, Sam, for never giving up. And thanks for teaching me a lesson or two.

Ask the Holy Spirit who He is wanting you to persistently love into an encounter with Him.

7.2

Home-inspired foreign policy sees the needy and cares for them.

I met them at church during the first week of school. Daniel, our Nepali friend, brought them. People are always more willing to go to church or some kind of event during the first few weeks of school because they are desperate to make friends. Many international students especially want to meet Americans. Their names were Namita and Manita. They seemed very sweet, and I invited them to come over and watch *Wonder Woman* at my house.

Weeks rolled by: the nap times, the endless laundry and dishes, the meal prep, eating, and cleaning never seemed to subside. The "just barely" connecting with my husband in between nursing a baby and wrangling and three-year-old also continued. It just never seemed very convenient to have these girls over and really engage with them. But I said I would, so after some time, I begrudgingly followed through. After several failed attempts and almost two months, we arranged for them to come over for dinner. The night they were coming, I considered cancelling because the kids had been rough that day and I didn't feel very well.

But we went ahead anyway.

They came in with Daniel smiling. They were so sweet and I'd forgotten how kind and gentle they were. They complimented us on our house, and I said the awkward, "Thanks, it's really been a blessing," knowing that in Nepal, most people sleep in the same room and houses are much smaller on average.

I took their coats, offered them something to drink, and started to engage.

I asked them about their impressions of the United States. I asked them about their plans and what they are going to do next semester, about their studies, and about their living situations.

We sat down to eat. I prayed. "Lord, bless these women and their endeavors and please make the food taste good. In Jesus' name. Amen." I like to add a little humor to the prayer because many of those who come from other nations haven't ever prayed to Jesus. They told me that the food (chicken curry) was amazing! Thank you, Lord, for giving me the wisdom about how to cook it!

Conversation then went a little deeper. I asked about Nepal and the systems and institutions in Nepal. They said it's very difficult to start a business in Nepal because of governmental red tape. This was interesting to me, so I asked them a little more about it.

I told them that this might be a strange question, but that I believe that every nation has a redemptive quality to add to the global community. I asked them what they thought Nepal added. They said Nepali people have a strong sense of community and communal living. I told them that was very precious. Daniel chimed in and said that was why it's hard to be a Christian because there is strong social pressure to conform to cultural norms within the community. The girls sounded surprised, so we talked about that a little more. The name Jesus was mentioned and I told them that I wasn't raised in a Christian home. They were fascinated by that idea, so I had the opportunity to tell them my story with Jesus. They said that many of their relatives were starting to follow Jesus, an indicator to me that God is fiercely on the move in Nepal. I smiled inwardly. These girls have been prayed for, I'm sure. And here they are.

We wrapped up after tea and little cookies and about two hours of eating and continual conversation. They thanked me again and again and then left. I later learned from Daniel that I was the first American who had ever had them over.

As I cleaned up the kitchen, I thought about how life giving that dinner was. It was truly delightful getting to know these women. The push to get there seemed almost insurmountable, but when we were actually in the middle of dinner, the grace was abundant! And I thought about God and how He is the God that sees.

He saw Hagar when she had been exiled from the people of promise. He saw Rahab in the midst of her squalor and rescued her. He saw Naomi and Ruth and blessed them beyond reason. And He sees these two Nepali women making their journey to America and endeavoring to improve their lives and the lives of their family and community back home. He is the God who sees. And He saw fit to bring them over to my place where I could be His "seeing" eyes by getting to know them, learning about their hearts and their lives. The power of being seen, really feeling seen, is greater than we realize. Simply by taking interest in another person, we validate and value their existence. We say, "You are worth stopping for." And that is a tangible means of transmitting God's unfathomable love.

We can stop a person on the street and tell them about Jesus, and many times a good seed is sown there. But when we take the time to really see a person and care about their lives, their circumstances, their challenges, and their passions, we model love to a whole different degree.

He is the God who knew them before the foundation of the world. He is the God who knit them in their mother's womb. He is the God who sees them and their nation and says they were worth dying for. When I stop the hamster wheel of my own life for such moments as these, God pours out His grace and peace and I partner with Him in His redemptive work of letting those who feel unseen know that He is the God who sees.

Ask the Holy Spirit to help you see those He is wanting you to see. Ask Him how to act upon those He has highlighted to you.

Final Thought

Those who aspire to build Home Inspired inherit the promises of God by abiding not striving.

I never thought of myself as a "doer." But when push comes to shove and something needs to change, I want to make a plan and **do** something to get it done. That sounds like a fairly benign way of responding to life, or maybe even a powerful way of responding, right? It's just that sometimes my doing is driven by fear and actually switches me into operating under the law instead of focusing on His grace and goodness to deliver promises in my life.

So sometimes, my doing gets frustrated by a good God who wants me to learn His distinct rhythms of grace.

When I think about it, a lot of my doing, especially if I'm feeling desperate and poor in any given area, is out of a desperation to make something happen because I'm convinced that nothing will happen unless I **make** it happen. It's a mentality that totally denies the presence and activity of a good God in my life.

My husband and I want to get pregnant again. Other than doing the "normal" doings that couples do, I'm monitoring my ovulations, my temp, seeing my doctor, getting blood drawn, etc. I'm doing things, but if I'm honest, I want to do more and constantly wonder if more is required to move this thing along. After waiting a while, I can start to feel desperate and believe lies about God's heart for me.

Meanwhile, I was reading the Word. I was reading in Genesis about the original design and the fall. It was so interesting to me that wrapped in each part of the curse was this futile "doing." God said that anything we put our hand to would be hard, arduous, and feel fruitless or at least feel like so much effort for meager benefits. Under the curse, the fruit of the doing would always be disappointing.

The contrast really struck me between a garden with all the resources, wisdom, and fellowship any person would ever want and the dry, lonely wasteland of the curse.

How often do I operate under the curse when Jesus took the curse for me? How often do I see myself in the wasteland instead of the garden? How often do I expect to strive and work and labor all on my own for something? Given my pledge to God so many years ago, I could understand why He might frustrate my plans. He paid a huge price for me to have something so much better.

He is wanting me to know that the curse has been broken. No longer are we under the works of the law, the striving and the doings without God. That is, unless we knowingly or unknowingly submit to that way again. The good news is we don't have to live that way. He made a way where there was no way for us to get back to the garden and to be rightful citizens there.

Of course, this concept applies not only in our desire to conceive but also with everyday parenthood. Where is my trust? Is it in my ability to be a perfect mom? Is my trust in my ability to give my kids the best attention, education, and upbringing? Because that is exhausting! Or is my trust in the promises of God? I want to walk in the way of love and model a life lived for Jesus before my children, but my choices to do that do not guarantee anything. It is only the promise of a faithful, all mighty God that is a guarantee. And my God promises to bless the righteous for one thousand generations after them. He promises that my children will be taught directly by Him. And on and on.

So, now when I "do," I want to keep in mind that I'm back in the garden by the blood of Christ. I'm free to sow and to design and to plan and to order things with Him. I'm set up to win! I've got all the resources and wisdom of a good God right at my fingertips. And where I end, He is only beginning. I can relax and enjoy the ride as I learn and discover what it means to work from redemption and wholeness and not for it, as I learn to walk in His distinct rhythms of grace.

And so, mom or mom-to-be, there's my prayer for you... that these words would impart grace and vision to you and empower you to go and make your home inspired. You work from redemption and wholeness, not for it. If you need wisdom, just ask and He will give it to you in generous proportions. This is your season. This is your moment. Don't miss it.

The Big Toe Is Dipped

As I write and edit this book, I'm well aware that there is much more to discuss. I know any one of these chapters could be expanded upon substantially. Hopefully there have been some thought-provoking moments for you as you've read through *Home Inspired*.

Here's my appeal.

I've only just barely dipped my big toe in the wisdom that God wants to download to our generation about home. It has to be fresh and it has to be God. In other words, while we have great treasures we can learn from older generations, we have to make it our own in this time in history. I'm not looking to be the star of the home-inspired movement. I'm looking to incite conversation and consideration as we look at this incredible micronation and how God can receive glory in and through it.

Do you have thoughts or insights about your own journey with home inspired? Would you send them to me?

Let's continue this journey together. Let's continue the conversation. Let's allow God to reveal His wonders and wisdom to us as we peer a little more intently into God's design for home.

Made in the USA
Lexington, KY
25 February 2019